BRAZILIAN JIU-JITSU
THE CLOSED GUARD

BJ PENN

DAVE CAMARILLO
ERICH KRAUSS & GLEN CORDOZA

LAS VEGAS

First Published in 2009 by Victory Belt Publishing.

ISBN 10: 0-9815044-6-9

ISBN 13: 978-0-9815044-6-9

This book is for educational purposes. The publisher and authors of this instructional book are not responsible in any manner whatsoever for any adverse effects arising directly or indirectly as a result of the information provided in this book. If not practiced safely and with caution, martial arts can be dangerous to you and to others. It is important to consult with a professional martial arts instructor before beginning training. It is also very important to consult with a physician prior to training due to the intense and strenuous nature of the techniques in this book.

Cover Design by Michael J. Morales, VIP GEAR

Printed in Hong Kong

CONTENTS

DRILLS

WARM-UP DRILLS AND EXERCISES

SUBMISSION DRILLS

CLOSED GUARD FUNDAMENTALS

BREAKING POSTURE

BASIC STRATEGY

CHOKES

ARM ATTACKS

STRAIGHT ARM BARS

KNEELING OPPONENT

OPPONENT WITH ONE LEG UP

OPPONENT STANDING

INVERTED ARM BARS

KIMURAS

AMERICANAS

OMOPLATA SETUPS

OMOPLATA CONTROL SUBMISSIONS

SWEEPS AND TRANSITIONS

"Who is this kid?" I thought to myself the first time BJ Penn grappled at Ralph Gracie's BJJ academy in Mountain View, California. He was sixteen years old, and his pidgin so thick I could hardly understand a word he said. Supposedly he had no jiu-jitsu experience to speak of, but here he was giving Big Mammoth one hell of a time on the mats.

Big Mammoth was the watchdog of the gym, the student Ralph unleashed on all newcomers. His job wasn't to pamper new students, but rather to dominate them. With the sport still in its infancy in America and self-proclaimed instructors popping up everywhere, it was our way of claiming, "our school is the best." Like me, Mammoth was one of Ralph's top blue belts. He was a beast on the mats, and I expected him to tear BJ up, but he was having serious trouble passing his guard. Having bought into the attitude of the day, I got upset with him. How could he be having trouble with this outsider?

But it wasn't just Mammoth. I obviously had a leg up on BJ due to a few years of jiu-jitsu and a lifetime of judo, but everyday I grappled with him, I had a harder time submitting him than the last. That's not normal. In jiu-jitsu, progression is usually measured in years. This kid literally got better every single day.

Not long after he came to us, I remember teaching a class in Modesto. I decided to show a particular guard pass, so I pulled BJ out into the center of the mats to demonstrate. Wanting to show the move's effectiveness, I told him to resist. That's just what he did, and I couldn't pass his guard. Being a very irresponsible instructor, I grew frustrated. I forgot that I was teaching and people were watching, and I spent the next twenty minutes trying to pass his guard. In the end, I failed. As a matter of fact, I never did pass his guard again.

A lot of people talk about BJ's flexibility and strength, and sure both of those attributes helped him advance and develop a mean closed guard. But it was more than that. He learned very quickly how to move his hips and relax. This is not easy to accomplish. Some jiu-jitsu practitioners relax too much, which allows them to get overwhelmed, and others don't relax enough, which causes them to quickly fatigue. BJ found that balance right off the bat, and soon he was playing with his opponents from the closed guard.

It also helped that Ralph had us tirelessly practice a passing drill from closed guard. It was pretty simple. If the guy on the bottom could sweep or submit his opponent, he won and got to remain on the bottom. If the guy on top managed to pass, he won and claimed the bottom position. It became very competitive, and BJ was determined to never relinquish his bottom spot. To accomplish this, he learned a broad array of techniques, most of which you will find in this book. If there wasn't a technique to accomplish what he wanted to accomplish, he invented it. I'm pretty sure he was only training at the Ralph Gracie academy at the time, yet he utilized moves I had never seen before.

Another reason BJ excelled so quickly at the closed guard is that he learned how to play the game. If one technique wasn't working, he moved on to something else. He became like an octopus—just when you thought you were about to open his guard, he was controlling your arms and breaking your posture. If you tried to stand, he threw off your base. And if by some fluke you did manage to stand, he would hang on to you like a monkey and continue to work for a sweep or finish from the closed guard.

This was Ralph Gracie's mentality—never open your guard unless your opponent is about to open it for you. Ralph would always shout at us, "Put him in your closed guard and don't let him out until you finish him." It forced us to see that the closed guard and open guard are two entirely different systems. Instead of transitioning mindlessly from closed guard to open guard in an attempt to get your offense going, you remained in closed guard and attacked with nonstop sweeps and transitions and submissions. This leads to one of two outcomes—either your opponent succumbs to your attacks or he achieves his goal and begins opening your guard. If you sense that your opponent is about to open your guard, that's when you shift to the open-guard system. Instead of letting him open your guard, you do so by your own will and immediately transition into an open-guard attack. If you allow him to open your guard, his agenda is being pushed. If you open your guard before he can attain that victory, your agenda is being pushed.

This mentality is what separated us from a lot of the other BJJ guys we saw at the tournaments. While they would relax and go to open guard, we maintained an aggressive closed guard. A nice by-product of this is that it allows you to conserve energy. The closed guard is the only bottom position where your opponent burns more energy than you do. Once you open your guard, it reverses. You burn more energy than

your opponent. The same goes for half guard and butterfly guard.

Developing an aggressive closed guard also helps if you plan on competing in mixed martial arts. In a fight, your opponent not only has guard passes on his side, but also an array of strikes. If you haven't spent time working on an aggressive closed-guard game, you won't be ready for that pressure. When training the closed guard, you don't want to see it is a tool for tournaments. Every time you play the closed guard, your goal should be to destroy your opponent.

This is what BJ did when he first got into MMA. When he got taken down in his second fight with Matt Hughes, he didn't take his time to settle—he flowed directly into an attack the instant his back hit the mat, pulled out his infamous octopus guard, and transitioned toward Matt Hughes's back. When he landed on his back in his first fight with Georges St. Pierre, he went right for the go-go plata choke.

This aggressiveness is demonstrated throughout this book. When playing the closed guard, instead of thinking you're in a disadvantageous position because your opponent is on top of you, see it for what it is—a trapped position for your opponent. If he attempts to posture up and create space, use the posture-breaking techniques to pull him back down on top of you. Space is your enemy. You want to keep him close, keep him bothered. Every second you want to be moving and attacking. The instant you rest, your opponent will have a chance to push his agenda. I realize that this might be tiring, but as long as you work on developing that fine balance of relaxation and tension, your opponent will burn more energy than you. If he defends one of your attacks, utilize his defense to transition into another. As you will soon see, this book covers dozens of these types of combinations.

And most of all, have fun.

-Dave Camarillo

ABOUT THIS BOOK

There are countless guard systems that can be utilized while grappling, ranging from the open guard, half guard, and butterfly guard to the more dynamic guard systems, such as the rubber guard, De La Riva guard, X-guard, and spider guard. Although learning and practicing each guard system will improve your game, the focus of this manual is on the most essential guard of them all—the closed guard.

While the closed guard is perhaps the most basic guard, it is the most important one to master. With your legs wrapped around your opponent's waist and your feet hooked together behind his back, you have substantial control of his body, which allows you to execute a broad array of submissions, sweeps, and transitions. In addition to having a great number of attacks, it is also a relatively safe position. There are very few finishing locks that your opponent can employ when trapped in your closed guard. To increase his offensive options, he must pry your legs apart, pass your guard, and establish a dominant position such as side control or mount.

This book is dedicated to the attacks that can be utilized from the closed guard. Instead of offering random groupings of techniques, I've broken the book down into sections. To begin, I demonstrate some basic drills that will help train your body and mind for the movements needed when playing closed guard. The more you practice these drills, the more fluid you will become with your attacks and transitions. Next, I dissect the importance of posture control and fundamental strategies. While training to break your opponent's posture might not be as entertaining as practicing submissions, it is a fundamental part of jiu-jitsu. As you will soon learn, if you are unable to control your opponent's posture, many of the closed-guard techniques in this book will not be available.

Next, I dive into attacks. The first attack section focuses on chokes, and the second section covers arm attacks. Both sections are broken down into multiple subsections. The choke portion covers collar chokes, arm chokes, and triangle chokes, and the arm attacks sections cover straight arm bars, inverted arm bars, and shoulder locks such as the kimura, Americana, and omoplata. In each of these subsections, you will not only learn how to apply the submission, but also several methods for setting up the finish. To conclude the book, I offer several sweeps and transitions that can be executed from closed guard.

It is important to note that although an entire subsection has been devoted to each specific attack, such as the straight arm bar and triangle, all the sections are interconnected. For example, if you apply a straight arm bar and your opponent defends against it, you can use his defense to transition into a triangle. If he defends against the triangle, you can use his defense to transition into an omoplata. I cover many of these types of transitions throughout the book, and it is important that you learn as many as possible. Remember, no attack works all of the time. In order to catch an experienced grappler in a finishing hold, you must become a master at stringing your attacks together in fluid combinations until you land a submission or execute a sweep. To help you along this path, I begin each subsection with a basic submission. As the subsection progresses, I show the same setup to that submission, but a different finish based upon your opponent's defensive reactions. With the techniques being laid out from simple to complex, I recommend studying the book sequentially.

With all of the techniques covered in this book, there is one thing I cannot stress enough—DON'T STALL. This is the most important concept to remember when fighting from the closed guard. Every moment you hesitate is another second your opponent has to attack with a pass. It is important to remember that you are stuck on the bottom, which means your opponent has superior leverage and can press his weight down on top of you. If you lie flat on your back and allow him to apply downward pressure, you will fatigue quickly and most likely get your guard passed. The instant you secure the closed guard, immediately employ your offense.

SECTION ONE
DRILLS

SHRIMP MOVE

As a rule of thumb, you never want to be flat on your back because it limits your mobility and allows your opponent to be highly offensive. If you should find your back pinned to the mat, the shrimp move is an excellent technique to utilize to get onto your side and create space between your opponent's body and your body. Once you have created that space, you want to immediately use it to execute an attack or, most often, a defensive movement. If you look at the photos below, you'll notice that as I use the shrimp move to turn onto my side, the distance between my knees and upper body shrinks. This is a much better defensive position than lying flat on your back, which separates your legs from your upper body and allows your opponent to put weight on you. To get familiar with this technique, it should be done as a warm up on a daily basis. When teaching, I'll have my students do the shrimp move across the length of the mat and then back again. In the beginning, it is important to take your time with each step to learn correct form, but eventually you'll want to flow from one shrimp to the next, down the mat and then back. If you take the time to master this technique, you'll be much more effective from the guard.

Lying flat on my back, I place my elbows on the mat next to my body and position my hands in front of my chest. At the same time, I plant my left foot on the mat near my left buttock so that my knee is pointing upward. Keeping my right leg flat to the mat, I point the toes of my right foot in the direction of my shrimp. In this case, I am going to shrimp to my right, so my toes are pointing to my right.

Driving off my left foot, I bridge my lower back to create space between my imaginary opponent and me. Now that my hips are elevated, it will be easy to turn my body and move onto my right side. Notice how I have kept my hands in front of me to prevent my imaginary opponent from dropping his weight down on me and hindering my movement.

Still using my hands to hold my imaginary opponent at bay, I turn onto my right side and scoot my hips toward my left to create space along my belt line. At the same time, I use my right knee to deflect my opponent's pressure, much like checking a kick in Muay Thai.

To create as much space as possible, I extend my arms into my opponent and continue to scoot my hips toward my left by driving off the mat using my left foot. In order to get the most out of this technique, continue to scoot your hips back until your left leg straightens and you can no longer push off the mat with your foot. It is also important to lock your arms straight to maintain the space you created. If your arms are bent, it becomes a battle between your muscles and your opponent's muscles. Even if you are stronger than him, he has his weight on his side, allowing him to overpower you. If your arms are locked straight, it becomes a battle between your bone structure and your opponent's muscle, making it much more difficult for him to close the gap. Once you have reached this position, you have completed the first shrimp move.

To continue with the drill and execute a shrimp move to the opposite side, I straighten my body, plant my elbows by my sides, position my hands over my chest, elevate my right knee, and flatten my left leg.

I execute the shrimp move to my right. From here, I will continue with the drill all the way down the mat and back.

KEY CONCEPTS

- The goal is to use your arms to catch your opponent's weight and push his body away from you, while at the same time scooting your body away from your opponent.
- Keep your body compact.
- Use your feet to generate power for the movement. This allows you to shrimp your body away from your opponent instead of just shrimping in place.

STANDING IN POSTURE

When you have an opponent in your guard, he has weight and leverage on his side, giving him a distinct advantage. While utilizing technique, movement, and push-and-pull are ways to level the playing field, you must possess the ability to escape from guard when your opponent shuts down your sweeps, submissions, and transitions. For this reason, the technique demonstrated in the sequence below is the most important technique in jiu-jitsu. It can be fun to learn all the new techniques fighters are putting out, but it you fail to focus on the fundamentals, your game will have massive holes. I strongly recommend practicing this drill every week. If you master it as you develop the other aspects of your guard, you will become very effective at fighting off your back. If you chose to ignore this fundamental technique and focus exclusively on the it-moves of the day, you will routinely get stuck between a rock and a hard place.

To assume the basic, postured guard position, I post my right hand on the mat behind me and assume a base grip (fingers and thumb spread out wide), straighten my right arm to keep my upper body elevated, post my left foot on the mat near my buttocks, flatten my right leg on the mat, and position my left hand in front of me to deflect my opponent's movements or grab his belt, leg, or collar. It is very important to notice that my upper body and head are not facing the same direction. While my head is facing my imaginary opponent, I have slightly turned my shoulders toward my right arm to strengthen my post and make my escape easier to manage. If you fail to turn your core toward your post, you will be in a weak position.

Deciding it is time to make the move to the standing position, I support my weight on my right hand and left foot and elevate my hips off the mat. Notice how I keep my left hand extended to serve as a range finder and keep my head facing my opponent.

With my hips elevated and only my two posts touching the mat, I begin to draw my right leg underneath my body.

I pull my right leg underneath my body and plant my foot on the mat behind my right hand. If you plant your foot in front of your base grip, you will most likely fall over. Once I achieve this tripod position, I have a solid base and can stand up.

I posture all the way up and position my hands for action. With my right knee slightly bent, I can shoot in for a takedown, back away, or circle around my opponent. From this hub position, I am also poised to deal with any attack, whether it be my opponent shooting in for my legs, jumping guard, or trying to engage in grip fighting.

ARM BAR DRILL

In order to be effective from the bottom guard position, you must be able to capitalize on every opportunity to attack, sweep, or stand. If a window opens and you fail to quickly jump through, you'll miss a chance to eliminate your opponent's leverage and weight. With the arm bar being one of the more effective submissions from the guard, it is important to drill it often to ingrain the movement into your mind. The goal is not to drill as fast as possible, but rather execute the movements slowly and with prevision. Focus on rotating your hips off to the side and applying downward pressure with your legs to prevent him from posturing up and escaping. Only after you have execute these movements fluidly should you increase your speed.

I begin the drill with my opponent in my closed guard. My feet are locked together behind his back, my hands are cupped around his elbows (no gi grip), and my head is elevated so I can see openings.

I unhook my feet and draw my legs toward my upper body. My left leg stays tight to Dave's right side while my right leg moves slightly away from his body. Notice how I have placed my right hand in front of Dave's left arm—this will help me turn my hips in a clockwise direction and lock in the submission.

Keeping my left leg wrapped around Dave's side, I apply downward pressure to keep his posture broken. I also use that pressure along with my hands to rotate my body in a clockwise direction. As I do this, I swing my right leg toward the right side of Dave's head. Notice how I'm using my hands to keep his arms tight together and to the inside of my legs.

With my upper body positioned off to the side and my hips perpendicular with Dave's hips, I wrap my right leg around the right side of his head. From here, I am in a perfect position to apply the arm bar, but for the sake of the drill, I will release my hold and assume this exact position on the opposite side.

I remove my right leg from the right side of Dave's head and begin to swing it toward the left side of his body.

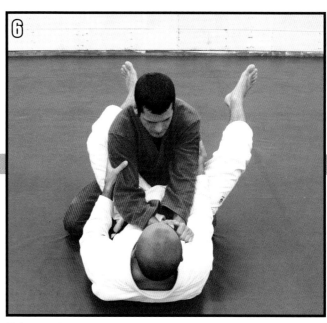

Using my hands and the momentum of my right leg, I rotate my hips in a counterclockwise direction.

I wrap my right leg around Dave's left side and apply downward pressure to keep his posture broken and help rotate my hips in a counterclockwise direction. At the same time, I swing my left leg toward the left side of his head. Again, notice how I'm using my hands to keep his arms together and to the inside of my legs.

With my upper body positioned off to the side and my hips perpendicular with Dave's hips, I wrap my left leg around the left side of his head. From here, I am in a perfect position to apply the arm bar, but for the sake of the drill, I will release my hold and assume this exact position on the opposite side.

TRIANGLE DRILL

The triangle is another high-percentage move from the guard, but in order to be effective with it, you must train your body to be fluid with its awkward movements. When conducting the drill, instead of focusing on applying pressure with your legs, concentrate on relaxing your upper back, lifting your hips, and then shifting your hips from side to side. It is also key to bridge your hips high into the air, which allows you to snare your opponent's head should he be postured up.

To assume the triangle position, I hook my right foot underneath the crook of my left leg and then arch my foot. Notice how my right knee is pointing toward the outside of my body and my left knee is pointing upward.

As I relax my legs and open my triangle, I drive my feet straight upward and then use that momentum to roll toward my upper back, lift my hips off the mat, and rotate my body in a clockwise direction.

As I drop my hips on my right side, I coil my right leg over my left foot. To assume the triangle position, I arch my left foot.

Again, I relax my legs and open my triangle. As I do this, I drive my feet straight upward and then use that momentum to roll toward my upper back, lift my hips off the mat, and rotate my body in a counterclockwise direction.

I assume the triangle position as I drop my hips toward my left side. When executing this drill, speed is important. Sometimes the triangle is only available for a brief moment, and in order to capitalize, the movements must be ingrained into your subconscious. It's a lot like sitting at a stoplight. The minute the green light comes on, you must be ready to step your foot on the gas and apply the triangle. If you have to think about what to do when the green light appears, it will often be too late.

NO-HANDED TRIANGLE DRILL

In this drill, you practice locking the triangle submission on your partner without using your hands to develop lower body control and coordination. Again, the goal is not to see how fast you can apply the submission, but rather work on developing perfect form. When conducting the drill, focus on keeping your upper body relaxed and using your legs to keep your opponent's trapped arm to the inside of his body.

I begin in the triangle position with my legs locked together. Since my right leg is underneath my opponent's left arm, I hook my right foot underneath my left leg. To make it difficult for my opponent to open my guard, I arch both feet.

I open my guard and drop my right foot to Dave's left hip. Next, I push off his left hip with my right foot, which makes it easier for me to curl my left leg into the back of his neck and force his head downward. Also, notice how I am using my right leg to force his left arm toward my left side.

I continue to curl my left leg into the back of Dave's neck to break his posture.

Once Dave's posture is broken, I elevate my right leg and move in front of my left foot.

I hook my right leg over my left foot, curl my right foot downward, and squeeze my knees together.

NO-HANDED OMOPLATA DRILL

To apply the omoplata shoulder lock, you trap one of your opponent's arms between your legs, and then use that position to break his posture. By drilling these actions without using your hands, your leg muscles will become conditioned and your movements more precise. Becoming a master at reaching the omoplata position is important because it not only opens up the omoplata shoulder lock, but also a number of other effective submissions.

I begin in the closed guard. To start the drill, my opponent reaches his right arm toward my left armpit. Although his intent is to establish control of my body, it will allow me to swing into the omoplata.

As Dave continues to reach his right hand toward my left armpit, he begins prying my legs apart using his right arm.

Relaxing my legs, I open my guard, pull my knees toward my head, and begin circling my left leg over Dave's right arm.

Continuing to rotate my body in a clockwise direction, I hook my left leg over the back of Dave's right shoulder and then drive my foot toward the mat. At the same time, I hook the crook of my right leg over my left foot.

As I drive my feet downward, Dave's head collapses to the mat. Notice how my actions have isolated his right elbow away from his body. Anytime you can force your opponent's arms away from his core, he is vulnerable to attack. If you were fighting instead of practicing a drill, this is where you would transition into the omoplata submission.

I open my guard, relieve the downward pressure I'm applying with my left leg, and begin regressing to the starting position.

I open my guard all the way. As Dave postures up, I drive my left leg into Dave's right side and use it as an anchor to rotate my body in a counterclockwise direction.

As I continue to rotate my body in a counterclockwise direction, Dave dives his left arm toward my right armpit. As he does this, I swing my right leg around the back of his left shoulder.

I swing my right leg around the back of Dave's left shoulder. Notice how my right heel is pointing toward the mat—the direction in which it will shortly head.

Still rotating my body in a counterclockwise direction so that I'm parallel to Dave, I begin driving my right foot toward the mat. Notice how this action immediately begins to shatter his posture.

I hook the crook of my left leg over my right foot. Next, I drive my left foot to the mat. From here, I will continue the drill by once again locking in the omoplata on the opposite side.

FUNDAMENTALS

CLOSED-GUARD FUNDAMENTALS

Before you dive into dynamic attacks such as arm bars, triangles, and sweep transitions, it is important to learn the basic strategies of the closed guard. If you bypass the fundamentals, the submissions and sweeps presented later in the book will be very difficult to pull off. To help you along this path, I begin the section by demonstrating several ways to break your opponent's posture when he sits up in your closed guard, and I conclude with some tricks that you can utilize to keep your opponent on the defensive. Later in the book, I will show how to use these techniques to set up fight-ending submissions, so it is very important that you master them before moving on.

BREAKING POSTURE

In order to be offensive from the closed guard, you must control the distance between you and your opponent. The majority of the time, your opponent will do everything in his power to posture up and create space between your bodies. Not only does this make it easier for him to avoid your submissions, but it also makes it easier for him to pin your hips to the mat and pass your guard into a more dominant position such as side control or mount. However, utilizing the posture-breaking techniques covered in this section allows you to pull your opponent down on top of you, eliminating space. Once accomplished, your hips are more mobile, allowing you to inch them up his torso and begin hunting for submissions such as arm bars and triangle chokes.

BASIC STRATEGY

When you have an opponent in your closed guard, he will most likely look for some type of control. Sometimes he will grab your sleeve and other times he will latch on to your lapel. If you allow him to establish these grips, he can effectively pin your hips to the mat, which, as you now know, limits your submission opportunities and makes it much easier for him to pass. To keep you from getting dominated in this fashion, I've included a few tricks that can be used to break your opponent's grips, as well as hinder him from establishing his grips. More often than not, these techniques will generate a reaction out of your opponent that you can use to set up an attack.

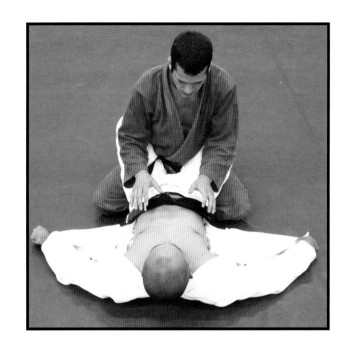

BREAKING POSTURE

If you've read the introduction to this section, then you already know that in order to attack your opponent from the closed-guard position you have to close the distance between your bodies. If you look at the photos in the sequence below, you'll notice that my opponent has latched on to my uniform and straightened his arms to keep my hips and shoulders pinned to the mat. To break past that barrier, I grab his elbows and pull them apart. Not only does this limit his offense and defense, but it also allows me to pull his body forward using my legs. To accomplish this, I spread my knees apart and swing my feet inward like a pendulum. If it doesn't work on the first try, I will do it again and again. The nice part about this technique is that your opponent exerts more energy with his defense than you do with your attack, which means he will tire first. Once I have him broken down, I immediately assume control of his head with my left arm and overhook his left arm with my right arm. From this control, I can effectively set up a submission or sweep attack.

As Dave postures up in my closed guard, he establishes a right grip on my collar and a left grip along my waistline. Before he can use his positioning to open my guard, I grip the seam of his sleeves slightly above his elbows.

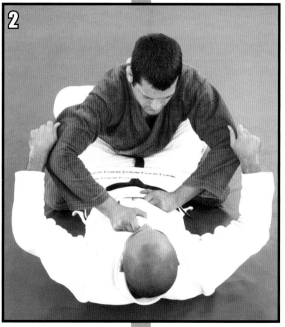

To break Dave's posture, I pull his elbows toward me and to the outside of my body as though I'm trying to put on a massive hat. At the same time, I angle my knees outward and draw my feet inward using my hip flexors to pull his body forward.

Continuing with my previous actions, I break Dave down into my guard. With his elbows now away from his body, his posture is weak, giving me an opening to attack. It is important to notice how my guard is extremely tight and I've pulled my feet toward my center.

Releasing my grips, I reach my left arm around the back of Dave's head and grip his left shoulder. Depending upon your preference, you can establish a grip on the shoulder seam of your opponent's gi or simply establish a palm grip in his armpit. The important part is that your arm is around your opponent's head and linked to his shoulder.

I wrap my right arm over Dave's left arm so our elbows are lined up, and then trap his arm to my side by sucking my elbow in tight to my body. At the same time, I tighten my left arm around his head. With my arms acting as straps that hold his body down, he will have a difficult time placing his hands on my chest and posturing up. From here, I will use the lack of space between our bodies to begin setting up submissions. Although stalling isn't the best tactic, if you need a quick rest, this is an excellent position from which to do it.

BREAKING POSTURE

INSIDE HEAD GRIP POSTURE BREAK

When your opponent is strong or has powerful grips, sometimes breaking his posture using the previous move is hard to manage. If you are unable to open his elbows using your hands, then attack his lead arm by turning onto your side, diving your arm underneath his lead arm, and then shooting your arm upward. As your arm elevates, it provides you with leverage and forces his arm toward the outside of your body. This not only shatters the primary pillar he is using to maintain his posture, but it also gives you access to his head. Just as before, you want to pull him down and immediately start hunting for a submission.

As Dave postures up in my closed guard, he establishes a right grip on my collar and a left grip along my waistline. Before he can use his positioning to open my guard, I grip his left sleeve with my right hand to relieve some of the pressure off my right hip and distract him from the coming move.

Maintaining my grip on Dave's right sleeve, I turn onto my right side, dig my left arm underneath his right arm, and then shoot my arm skyward. The goal is to drive your elbow into the crook of your opponent's arm. This forces his arm toward the outside of your body and shatters his post.

As Dave's right arm collapses, I angle my knees outward and draw my feet inward, pulling him forward. At the same time, I continue to reach my left arm upward and around the back of his head. Notice how I have maintained my right grip on his left sleeve. This is important because it prevents him from establishing a new lead post with his left arm.

To completely break Dave's posture, I pull him forward with all four limbs. Immediately I wrap my left arm tight around the back of his head and establish a grip on his left armpit.

With Dave broken back down in my closed guard, I wrap my right arm around his left arm. Once accomplished, I have both sides of his body controlled, making it difficult for him to push off my chest and create space. From here, I will launch my attack.

BREAKING POSTURE

WHIZZER CONTROL POSTURE BREAK

If your opponent is determined to stay postured up in your guard, it can be quite difficult to break him down, making it important to have more than one technique in your arsenal to achieve your goal. In this scenario, you dive your arm underneath your opponent's near arm and pull him forward using your legs, just as you did in the previous technique. However, instead of reaching up to control his head, you wrap your arm over his arm, establishing an overhook, or whizzer. This allows you to control his arm above his elbow, which makes it difficult for him to lift his head and posture. The other nice part about gaining control of your opponent's arm as you break him down is that you can use that control to help set up a submission. When attacking from guard, you never want to do so head on—you always want to attack from one side of your opponent's body or the other. By controlling one of his arms, it makes this task much easier to accomplish. The key to being successful with this technique is not releasing your sleeve grip until you have secured his arm with the overhook. If you let go too early, your opponent will be able to pull his arm free. Although this method for breaking posture can be viewed as superior to the ones I've already offered due to the options it opens up, it is important not to overlook the others. Once you've used a technique on your opponent, he will most likely be quicker to defend against it the next time you utilize it. To keep him guessing, chain the various posture breaking techniques together. If he defends against one, move right into another. Eventually, you'll find his weak spot and succeed.

Dave postures up in my guard, and I secure elbow control.

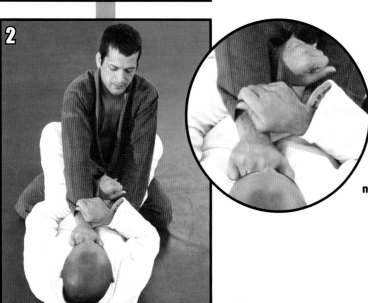

I grab Dave's right sleeve with my right hand, establishing a cross grip. At the same time, I slide my left arm underneath his right arm.

Turning slightly onto my right side, I shoot my left arm upward and pull Dave's right sleeve toward the left side of my head using my right hand, shattering his grip. The goal is to get my left elbow above his right elbow so I can control it. To help accomplish this, I widen my knees and draw my feet inward, pulling him forward.

Still pulling Dave inward using my legs, I turn more onto my right side and continue to extend my left arm upward until my elbow is above his elbow. At the same time, I pull my cross sleeve grip over and behind my head. Notice how my right arm is bent, and my right elbow is positioned behind my left shoulder.

Having pulled Dave into me using my legs and right sleeve grip, I wrap my left arm around his right arm, dig my hand underneath his right armpit, and then clamp down tight. After I have cemented his arm to my body, I release my right cross grip on his sleeve and grab his right lapel with my right hand. It is important to note that in order to secure a tight hold on your opponent's arm, your overhook must be positioned above his elbow. If your overhook is weak or you release your sleeve grip too early, your opponent will be able to pull his arm free.

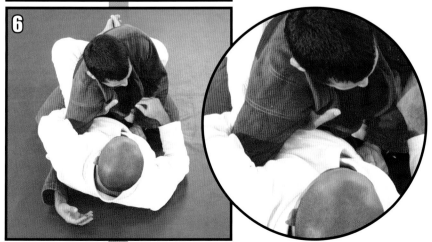

I pass Dave's right collar from my right hand to my left hand, which allows me to lock his right arm tighter to my body. With Dave's posture broken and one side of his body controlled, I will now use my free hand to begin setting up a submission.

GRIP TEASE

When an opponent postures up in your closed guard, he will most likely work to establish solid grips on your gi. In addition to helping him maintain his posture, these grips allow him to pin your back to the mat, which helps him achieve his goal of passing your guard into a more dominant position. To prevent an opponent from establishing these grips, I'll often bait him with my sleeve the instant he postures up. To entice him and make him believe that I'm unaware of my mistake, I'll look in the opposite direction of my sleeve. When he goes to grab it, I'll quickly pull my sleeve away. Sometimes my opponent will grow frustrated and abandon the idea of establishing a sleeve grip, and other times he will extend his body forward and reach for it, making him vulnerable to submissions. Even if your opponent doesn't take the bait, you will most likely distract him from his primary mission of passing and keep him locked in your closed guard longer. This works to your advantage because the longer you can keep your opponent in your closed guard, the more opportunities you have to catch him with a submission.

Dave has postured up in my guard, but he has not yet established a grip. To prevent him from establishing a right grip, I place my left hand on his right wrist and prepare to shove it downward. To distract him from establishing a left grip, I position my right arm across my torso to bait him into gripping it.

Dave takes the bait and reaches his left hand toward my right sleeve. As his fingers draw close, I begin pulling my right arm toward the back of my head.

Realizing Dave is determined to establish a grip on my right sleeve, I pull my arm back and place my hand behind my head, causing him to lean forward. At the same time, I draw my legs inward to further break him down. With his body extended forward, I can attack a number of different ways, including with a triangle choke or an arm bar.

OPENING THE GI

As I mentioned in the previous introduction, your opponent will most likely attempt to establish solid grips on your uniform when he postures up in your closed guard. By opening your gi, you prevent him from establishing those grips, making it difficult for him to execute a lot of the guard-opening techniques in his arsenal. This technique can also be used when your opponent has already established his grips. By grabbing your lapels slightly above his hands, and then ripping your gi outward toward the opening of his hands, you can break his grips in one simple movement. Once you have moved your lapels to the outside of your body, the next step is to angle your knees outward and pull your opponent forward using your legs. This gives him a couple of options. He can post his hands on your ribcage, but with nothing solid to hold on to, you can easily remove those posts by grabbing his sleeves and pulling. His other option is to plant his hands in your armpits to keep your body pinned, slide a knee between your legs, and then stand, but such a tactic can easily be countered by deflecting his grips with your elbows. The key to being successful with this move is using both your arms and legs. If you rip your lapels away from your body but forget to draw your opponent forward using your legs, you're giving him a chance to get offensive. Remember, any time you remove your opponent's ability to establish grips and post, you have an easy route to breaking him down into your closed guard.

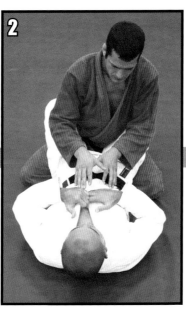

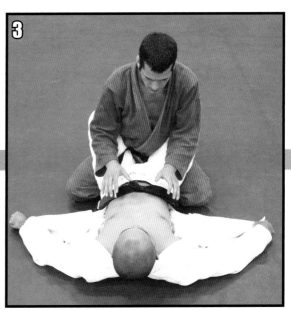

Dave has postured up in my guard, but he has not yet established his grips.

As Dave reaches to establish a grip, I grab my lapels in the middle of my chest and begin to open my gi.

I rip my gi open and spread my lapels out to my sides, eliminating Dave's potential grips. At the same time, I draw my legs inward to break his posture. From here, he has the option to reach forward and establish grips in my armpits, but it will require him to lean forward, which will allow me to attack or break his posture.

CHOKES

CHOKES

In this section, I cover the majority of chokes that are available from the closed guard, including collar chokes, arm chokes, and triangle chokes. Although each choke is set up differently, they all share the same goal—to cut off the blood flow to your opponent's brain. This is accomplished by pinching your opponent's carotid arteries, which are located on each side of his neck next to his trachea. When applied properly, your opponent's only choices are to quickly tap in submission or pass out. Chokes are very powerful submissions, but people tend to make a few crucial mistakes. The first mistake is to put all your power into the choke right off the bat, which often leads to fatigue and eventual failure. The second mistake is to apply pressure in spurts, which supplies your opponent's brain with intermittent blood flow and allows him to remain conscious. The key to applying a correct choke is not power, but rather constant pressure. To be effective, you must turn into a snake, making your strangle gradually stronger with each second that passes.

COLLAR CHOKES

Using your opponent's uniform to apply a choke is a highly effective way to achieve a quick finish. With each of the collar chokes presented in this section, it is very important to secure a deep initial first grip. This allows you to position the blade of your wrist against one of your opponent's carotid arteries. Your second grip is also important, but because it is primarily used to stabilize the position, it usually doesn't have to be as deep. Once you have established your grips, crossing your arms in front of your opponent's neck will pull either your wrist or his collar into his carotid arteries, severing blood flow to his brain. Although there are a lot of defenses for collar chokes, they are excellent for setting up other attacks. As you will see, your opponent's defenses against a collar choke can present an op-

portunity to make a quick transition into a triangle or an arm bar. Remember, nothing works a hundred percent of the time. In order to be effective from the guard, you must string your attacks together. For the best results, each transition you make should be based upon your opponent's reaction to the previous attack. For example, if you apply a collar choke, one of the most common defenses is for your opponent to grip his hands around his lapel to relieve pressure. This makes it difficult to finish the choke, but with your opponent's hands tied up with defense, you have a clear pathway to another submission. Later in the book, I will demonstrate a number of highly effective transitions based upon your opponent's choke defense, but first it is important to become a master at applying the various chokes. After all, if you don't threaten your opponent with your initial attack, he won't commit to his defense, which limits the follow-up attacks that you can apply.

ARM CHOKES

Arm chokes include guillotines and arm triangles. While collar chokes can be set up when there is distance between you and your opponent, arm chokes must be set up when you have body-to-body contact. For example, in order to set up a guillotine choke when your opponent is postured up, you must sit up into him, closing off all space between your bodies. This allows you to wrap your arm around the back of his head and then apply pressure by extending your arm upward into his neck. The same is true with the arm triangle, which is set up when your opponent secures the head and arm position. In addition to learning how to close off all space, it is also important to get onto one side of your body when applying arm chokes. If you attempt to finish an arm choke while lying flat on your back, not only will the submission most likely fail, but you will also burn precious energy, causing fatigue.

TRIANGLE CHOKES

In this section I demonstrate several ways to establish the triangle position by trapping your opponent's head and one of his arms between your legs. However, it is important not to view this position solely as a route to the triangle submission. Although the triangle submission is the most common way to finish your opponent from the triangle position, it's not always an option. If your opponent is experienced, he will most likely be armed with several ways to defend against the triangle. Instead of giving up on the position when your opponent blocks the triangle submission, use his defense to transition into another submission. As you will see, the triangle position is a gateway to a slew of highly effective offensive techniques. Due to the large number of alternate finishes, I've included them in their own section.

FINISHING FROM THE TRIANGLE POSITION

When you establish the triangle position, you not only gain access to your opponent's neck, but also his trapped arm. Should the choke fail, you can apply wrist locks, straight arm bars, and shoulder locks. With a number of highly effective options at your disposal, the triangle position should be viewed as a control position instead of as a setup to a single submission. And as with any control position, there should be rhyme and reasons to your actions. As you will see, most of the techniques presented in this section are based upon your opponent's reaction to the triangle control position. However, to prevent your opponent from escaping your control, you must identify which transition goes with which counter. The goal is to threaten him with the triangle submission, and then with every reaction he makes, you put him into deeper water. Like the saying goes, "out of the frying pan and into the fire." Just when he thinks he's escaping one attack, he falls into another.

BASIC GI CHOKE

This is an excellent submission to apply when you are unable to break your opponent's posture using one of the previous techniques. Instead of giving up, you lock in a basic gi choke. In addition to threatening him with a submission, the mechanics of the choke also allows you to break him down into your guard. If you look at the photos in the sequence below, you'll notice that I set up the choke by opening my opponent's lapel with one hand and then grabbing it with my other. This is key for establishing a deep grip, which is required for the choke to work. It also gives me great control of my opponent's upper body. Even if you aren't able to finish your opponent with this submission, you usually accomplish two very important tasks: You break his posture, and you threaten him. Anytime you are on bottom, you must threaten your opponent to prevent him from pushing his agenda. The longer you can keep your opponent on the defense, the more likely he will be to make a mistake.

Dave has postured up in my guard and established solid grips on my gi. Unable to break his posture using the previous techniques, I decide to apply a basic gi choke, which will threaten him and break his posture at the same time.

I grab Dave's left collar with my right hand and open it to create slack. At the same time, I cross my left arm over the top of his right arm. It is important to note that if you fail to open your opponent's gi, it will often be too taut to establish a deep grip. If you attempt the choke with a weak, shallow grip, it will most likely fail.

Instead of driving my body into Dave's right post, I drop my right shoulder down to the mat and elevate my left shoulder. As my body turns onto its side, Dave's right hand slides down my chest toward the mat. This allows me to reach my left hand higher and establish a deep grip on his collar behind his neck. For the best grip possible, I keep my thumb to the outside of his collar and slide my fingers inside his collar. Again, if your grip is too low on your opponent's collar, the choke will not be effective.

Once I have a solid left grip on Dave's collar, I release my right grip on his collar. With my right palm facing me, I immediately begin reaching my right hand underneath my left arm. If I had reached my right hand over my left arm, I would have established a different grip and gone for a different choke. To see this variation, flip to the next technique.

Just as I did with my left grip, I slide the fingers of my right hand under Dave's right collar and keep my thumb to the outside. With both of my grips deep, I turn the blades of my wrists into the sides of Dave's neck and cross my arms over one another to tighten the choke.

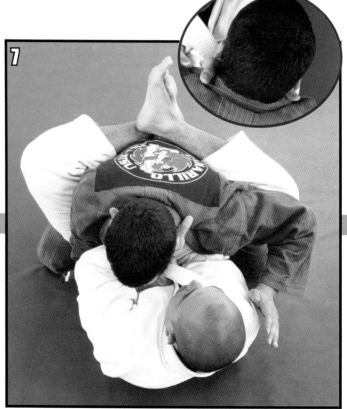

Using my grips, I pull Dave's body into me and bend my arms at the elbows. With my arms positioned in front of his arms, the collapse of my elbows forces his elbows to also collapse, breaking his posture. It is important to mention that your elbows should remain close to your sides. Do not let them stray outward or upward.

To lock in the choke, I turn the blades of my wrists into Dave's neck, slide my elbows along my ribcage toward the mat, and keep my legs tight. As my wrists cut into his carotid arteries, severing blood flow to his brain, he quickly taps.

BASIC GI CHOKE (THUMB DOWN)

A lot of times when you employ the previous basic gi choke, you'll establish your first grip, but then your opponent will block your free hand as you attempt to slide it underneath your arm, preventing you from establishing your second grip. Instead of giving up on the choke, immediately reach your free hand over your arm and establish a thumb-down grip on your opponent's collar. The same thing works in reverse. If you attempt the thumb-down choke first, and your opponent blocks your hand from reaching over your arm, drop your free hand low and slide it underneath your arm. In the first scenario, your opponent is blocking you low, so you switch your tactics and go high, and in the second scenario, your opponent is blocking you high, so you go low. The more fluid you are at combining these two techniques, the better chance you'll have of finishing your opponent.

Dave postures up in my guard and establishes a right grip on my lapel and a left grip on my waistline.

I grab Dave's left lapel with my right hand and pull it open to create slack. At the same time, I reach my left hand toward his left collar.

I drop my right shoulder to the mat and elevate my left shoulder. This causes Dave's right grip to slide down my chest toward the mat, allowing me to establish a left collar grip behind his neck. It is important to notice that my fingers are positioned to the inside of his gi, while my thumb is positioned on the outside.

Once my left grip is tight, I reach my right hand over my left arm. Notice how my palm is pointing toward my right.

I hook my thumb to the inside of Dave's right collar.

Once my right thumb is caught in Dave's collar, I slide it behind his neck and then grip the outside of his collar with my fingers. As you can see, the choke is already starting to disrupt his posture.

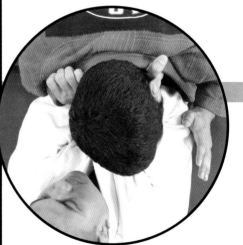

With my arms positioned in front of Dave's arms, collapsing my elbows also cause his elbows to collapse, breaking his posts on my body. At the same time, I widen my knees and draw my feet inward, forcing him forward into my guard.

I cross my arms. This forces the blade of my left wrist into the left side of Dave's neck and the bottom of my right wrist into the right side of his neck. By sliding my elbows down my ribcage, I create a vise that severs the blood flow to his brain. It is important to mention that your elbows MUST be tight to your sides. Do not let them stray outward or upward.

POSTURE UP TO GI CHOKE

In the previous two techniques, I secured my first grip, got my second grip, broke my opponent down, and then applied the choke. In this technique, I secure my first grip, break my opponent down, get my second grip, and then apply the choke. As I mentioned earlier, it's good to constantly switch techniques to keep your opponent guessing. Breaking him down before getting your second grip will often catch him off guard, especially because he can't see what you're doing with your free hand. This technique also comes in handy when your opponent senses the choke coming after you've established your first grip and drops his weight down on top of you in defense. Instead of giving up on the choke, you acquire it using a different method. I strongly suggest spending some time with this technique because learning how to take advantage of your opponent's positioning is just as important when he is broken down as when he is postured up.

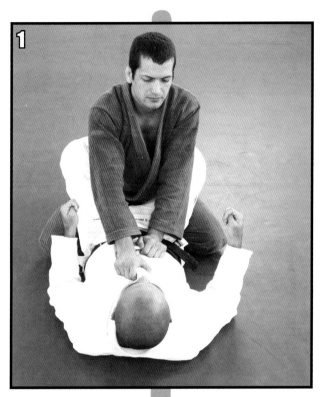

As Dave postures up in my guard, he establishes a right grip on my collar and a left grip along my waistline.

Dropping my right shoulder to the mat and elevating my left shoulder, I reach my left arm in front of Dave's right arm and grab his left collar with my thumb on the outside and my fingers on the inside. Notice how by turning onto my side I'm able to get more reach out of my left arm.

To get more extension out of my left arm so I can establish a deep grip on Dave's collar, I post on my right elbow and elevate my hips off the mat.

Keeping my hips elevated off the mat, I pull Dave into my chest using my left hand, breaking his posture.

I drop to my back and pull Dave with me using my left arm and legs. The instant I come down, I dig the thumb of my right hand underneath his collar behind his head.

With my thumb still dug underneath Dave's collar behind his head, I wrap the fingers of my right hand around the outside of his collar. Once I've secured a tight grip, I begin sliding my right arm over the top of his head. At the same time, I pull on his left collar with my left hand and force his head toward his right using my left forearm. Notice how these actions create an opening on the right side of his neck.

I slide my right arm over Dave's head and then position the blade of my wrist underneath his jaw. Notice how both of my elbows are tucked tight to my body. This allows me to apply more pressure with the choke.

Pulling Dave into me using my legs and arms, I slide my elbows down my ribcage toward the mat. This drives the blades of my wrists into his neck, cutting off blood flow to his brain.

COLLAR CHOKE (SHALLOW GRIP)

This choke is a little different from the previous ones in that the majority of pressure is applied to your opponent's trachea instead of his carotid arteries. Although it doesn't provide the same immediate results as when you sever the blood flow to your opponent's brain, it doesn't require you to completely break his posture, which is a nice attribute. A lot of times your opponent will attempt to block the choke by dropping his chin to his chest, but this can be prevented by driving the blade of your forearm into the contour of his jawline. If he manages to drop his chin before you can accomplish this, you don't necessarily want to give up on the choke. Even if your forearm is positioned over his chin, as you break him down into your guard, your arm will crank his head to the side, creating an opening under his chin that allows you to finish the choke.

As Dave postures up in my guard, he establishes a right grip on my collar and a left grip along my waistline.

I grab Dave's left collar with my right hand and open his gi.

Using my right hand, I pull Dave's left collar toward the outside of his body to create an opening for my left hand.

I slide my left thumb to the inside of Dave's left collar and then wrap my fingers around the outside of his collar, securing a tight grip. Next, I drive the blade of my left arm into his trachea, reach my right hand underneath my left arm, and establish a shallow grip on his right lapel using my right hand. It is important to note that for this choke you do not need to establish a deep grip with your right hand. All you're looking for is a handle that will allow you to tighten the gi around your opponent's neck and increase the leverage of your left arm.

I drive my left elbow upward, forcing the blade of my left forearm into Dave's trachea. As my action cranks his head toward his right side, I pull down on his right collar using my right hand to tighten his gi around his neck and increase the leverage of my left arm. Although Dave manages to maintain some of his posture, his gi is digging into his carotid arteries on both side of his neck, and my left forearm is digging into his trachea. This is a rougher choke than those previously shown.

CLOSED-GUARD COLLAR CHOKE

In this technique you do not attack your opponent's neck while he is postured up. Instead, you attack his lead post, gain control of his head, and pull him down on top of you. Since you're not threatening him with a submission, this is usually much easier to manage. However, while in the process of breaking him down, you grab his far lapel with your free hand. Worried about the big picture, most of the time your opponent won't even notice. Once you have him broken down, you wrap his lapel over his back and pass it off to the same hand you're using to control his head. This not only prevents him from posturing up, but it also allows you to set up the choke. As with all chokes, it is important to read your opponent's reactions once you have it locked in. If he is resisting and gurgling, there is a good chance he's on his way to tapping. However, if he is relaxed and stationary, he's probably doing a good job defending against it. Instead of holding on to the choke, which will cause your arms to quickly burn out, a better option is to use your positioning to transition to another submission.

As Dave postures up in my guard, he establishes a right grip on my collar and a left grip along my waistline. Realizing that if I apply a direct choke he will most likely defend against it, I decide to apply an indirect choke. To begin, I grab the bottom of his left lapel with my left hand and reach my right hand underneath his left arm.

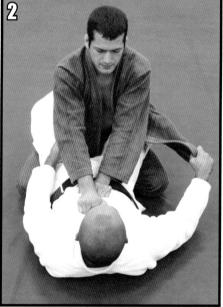

I pull Dave's left lapel out of his belt using my left hand, feed it to my right hand, and then pull his lapel away from his body. Notice how I have positioned my right thumb inward to increase my pulling power.

I continue to pull Dave's left lapel toward my right side, disrupting his balance. At the same time, I turn onto my right side and shoot my left arm underneath his right arm, breaking his lead post.

I shoot my left arm straight up, turning more onto my right side to extend my reach. As I continue to disrupt his balance by pulling his lapel toward my right side, it is difficult for him to defend against my actions.

Having attacked Dave's posture with both arms, his base is weakened. To capitalize, I wrap my left arm around his head and pull him downward. Keeping my left elbow tight to his body, I work to secure the position by feeding his lapel from my right hand to my left.

I pass Dave's left lapel to my left hand to keep his posture broken.

I reposition my right arm to the right side of Dave's head and then feed his left collar from my left hand to my right.

I pass Dave's left lapel from my left hand to my right. Notice how I establish my grip so that my palm is facing toward me and the blade of my right wrist is digging into the side of his neck underneath his chin.

I reach my left arm over my right arm and grab the shoulder of Dave's gi with my palm facing away from me. It is important to notice that my thumb is on the outside of his collar, not on the inside. With Dave's head positioned in the center of the X I formed with my arms, I am ready to apply the choke.

I draw my elbows in tight to my body and then slide them down my ribcage. As Dave is pulled downward, the blades of my wrists dig into his carotid arteries and sever the blood flow to his brain. It is important to notice that my head is to the right of Dave's head, which allows me to draw my right arm into the side of his neck with maximum force. Although my left grip is important, its primary function is to stabilize the pressure on the neck. Because my right arm is underneath, it is the primary choking instrument.

SIT-UP GUILLOTINE

This is an excellent technique to use when an opponent postures up in your guard and you're having no luck with the traditional chokes. By sitting up into him and executing a sweep, he will most likely defend by driving his weight into you to pin your back to the mat. Although this defense hinders you from executing the sweep, it allows you to transition right into a guillotine choke. However, there are a few things you must accomplish in order to be successful with this combination. The first is committing to the sweep. The goal is to execute the sweep with enough speed and power that your opponent will get swept to his back if he doesn't defend. Secondly, you must reach your elbow past your opponent's head when you sit up. This might seem difficult to accomplish if your opponent's posts on your body are extremely strong, but the nice part about this technique is that you don't confront his straightened arms head-on when sitting up. Instead, you turn onto your side, causing his grips to slide down your chest. Reaching your elbow past his head allows you to easily wrap your arm around his head as he defends, leading to a quick transition. Once you've wrapped up his head, it is also important to cup your palm over his chin and pull his head into your armpit, both of which hinder him from popping his head out of the trap.

As Dave postures up in my guard, he establishes a right grip on my collar and a left grip along my waistline.

Rotating my shoulders in a clockwise direction, I post my right elbow on the mat behind me and reach my left hand up and over Dave's left shoulder.

Continuing to reach my left arm over Dave's left shoulder, I open my guard, plant my feet on the mat, and push myself up to my right hand. Next, I use my feet and right hand to elevate my hips into Dave.

Reaching my left arm deeper over Dave's back, I relax my right leg, push off my left foot, and drive my hips forward and toward my right side. Notice how these actions begin to disrupt his base.

Realizing he is about to get swept to my right, Dave hugs my body and begins driving his weight forward to pin my back to the mat. To use his reaction to my advantage, I wrap my left arm around the back of his head and the right side of his neck.

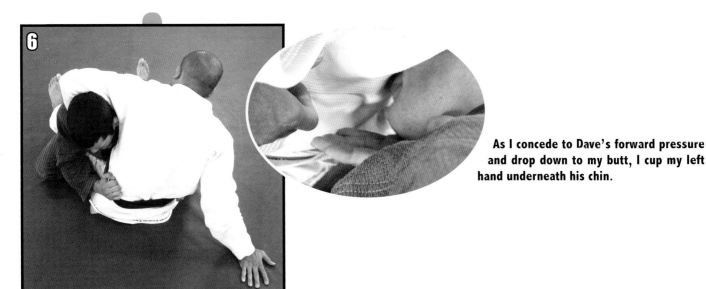

As I concede to Dave's forward pressure and drop down to my butt, I cup my left hand underneath his chin.

As Dave drives forward, I slide my right hand in front of his left arm and grab the back of my left hand. It is important to note that my left hand is underneath his chin, my left elbow is clamped down tight on the side of his head, and my right elbow is pointing as high as possible to add strength to the strangle.

As Dave drives me to my back, I fall onto my left hip, slightly shrimp my hips toward my right, close my guard, stretch my legs out to pull his body away from me, and use my right hand to force the blade of my left hand up into his throat. If you keep your hips square with your opponent instead of getting onto your hips and shrimping out to the side, it will be much harder to finish the choke. Also, notice how my left elbow is clamped tight, preventing him from pulling his head out from underneath my armpit, and the point of my right elbow is angled upward to add pressure to the choke.

ARM TRIANGLE

When you have an opponent in your closed guard and he's ahead on points, a lot of times he will drive into you, establish head and arm control, and attempt to stall his way to victory. To prevent him from achieving his goal, you can use his broken posture to capture him in an arm triangle. To be successful with this technique, it is important to establish strong grips on his gi. If you look at the first photo in the sequence below, you'll notice that I grab the back of his gi with my left hand. Not only can you use this grip to create the space needed to pull his arm over your head, but you can also use it to prevent him from posturing up, which is one form of defense against the choke. For the strongest grip, you want to position your thumb on the outside of his collar. Once everything is in place and you've applied the arm triangle, your opponent will have to focus on defending against the submission rather than passing your guard, which allows you to open your guard. This serves two purposes—it allows you to relax your legs and it makes for an easier transition to his back should the choke fail.

Instead of posturing up, Dave remains broken down in my guard and assumes head and arm control. To use his positioning to my advantage, I grab the seam running along his upper back using my left hand and latch on to his left elbow seam with my right hand. Notice that on both grips I have not involved my thumb.

Using my left grip, I push Dave's upper body slightly away from me to create the space I need to maneuver his left arm over my head using my right grip on his sleeve. However, if he were to suddenly attempt to posture up, I would use my left grip to pull him back into me. If you allow your opponent to posture up, you will lose the submission.

Having repositioned Dave's left arm to the left side of my head, I release my right grip on his sleeve and drive my head into his triceps. At the same time, I wrap my left arm tight around the right side of his head. The goal with this technique is to trap your opponent's arm against the side of his neck, and the only way to accomplish this is to apply pressure from both sides.

Still driving my head into Dave's left triceps, I press my left biceps into the right side of his head and reach my left hand upward. This gives me more length with my left arm and will allow me to close off the triangle. However, it is important to note that this step should be done very fast. If you take your time, your opponent will have a chance to posture up and escape the submission.

I wrap my left arm tightly around the back of Dave's head. Notice how this drives his left arm into the side of his neck.

I grab my right biceps with my left hand and then cup my right hand on Dave's forehead. To finish the submission, I squeeze everything tight and draw my elbows together. With my left arm digging into the right side of his neck and his left arm digging into the left side of his neck, blood flow is severed from his brain, forcing him to tap. It is also important to notice that I have opened my guard. If Dave should defend against the choke, I could make a quick transition to his back.

INSIDE HEAD GRIP TO TRIANGLE

In this technique I demonstrate a simple yet highly effective way to capture your opponent in a triangle choke when he postures up in your guard. The nice part about the technique is that it doesn't require you to grab your opponent's gi, making it applicable in both MMA and no-gi grappling competition. As you will see, the move involves breaking your opponent's posture and obtaining wrist control. Once both of these tasks have been accomplished, it is important to use your legs as feelers to quickly assess the situation. If you sense that your opponent is in the process of breaking your wrist control, opening your guard and transitioning to the triangle isn't the best idea because it can actually aid his task of passing your guard. In such a scenario, it's better to abandon the triangle and set up another submission.

As Dave postures up in my guard, he establishes a right grip on my collar and a left grip along my waistline. To keep my options open, I immediately grab his left sleeve with my right hand and his right sleeve with my left hand.

Maintaining my right grip on Dave's left sleeve, I slide my left arm underneath his right post and then shoot my arm upward. It is important to note that if you are grappling without a gi, grab your opponent's wrist instead of his sleeve.

As I shoot my left arm upward, I break Dave's lead grip. To capitalize, I quickly wrap my left arm around the back of his head and pull him into me.

As I break Dave down, I open my guard. Still with a tight right grip on his left sleeve, I force his left arm between my legs. When executing this step, it is important to maintain constant downward pressure on your opponent's head to prevent him from posturing back up. It is also important to notice how I move my right leg over the point of his left elbow and toward his shoulder.

Continuing to shove Dave's left arm between my legs, I move my right leg farther up his left arm.

As I release my right grip on Dave's left wrist, I wrap my right leg across the back of his head and apply downward pressure.

I throw my left leg over my right foot to establish the triangle position. To prevent Dave from posturing up, I curl my left leg downward, increasing the pressure of my right leg on his head and shoulder.

In order to finish the triangle, I need to move Dave's right arm to the right side of my body. To gain access to his arm, I bridge my hips upward.

I grab Dave's right arm with my left hand and move it to the right side of my body. The instant I accomplish this, I drop my hips and then crunch my upper body toward my legs to trap his arm across his neck.

To finish the submission, I coil my left leg down into my right leg and pull Dave's head down using both of my hands. With my right leg digging into the left side of his neck and his right arm digging into the right side of his neck, blood flow is severed from his brain, forcing him to tap.

TIGHT-SIDE-LIFT TRIANGLE / KIMURA OPTION

In the previous sequence, you broke your opponent down into your closed guard and shoved his wrist between your legs, allowing you to throw your leg over his shoulder and apply a triangle choke. This sequence is the exact same set of movements, but when you go to shove your opponent's wrist toward your groin, he defends by forcing his arm away from his body. Instead of fighting his resistance, you go with his movement and force his arm away from his body. Although this hinders you from throwing your leg over his arm, it allows you to pull your leg underneath his arm and apply the triangle. Once accomplished, you have a couple of finishing options. In the first finishing sequence, I finish with a regular triangle choke. However, sometimes you will find yourself up against an opponent who is a master at triangle defense. Instead of burning out your legs trying to finish the triangle, you keep his body trapped with your legs, pull your body off to his side, and attack his far shoulder with a kimura. It's an excellent option to have in your arsenal when the end of the match is near and your opponent is doing everything in his power to survive the triangle.

As Dave postures up in my guard, he establishes a right grip on my collar and a left grip along my waistline. To set up my attack, I grab his left sleeve with my right hand and begin sliding my left arm underneath his right arm.

I turn onto my right side and shoot my left arm upward. When executing this step, it is important to line your elbow up with your opponent's elbow. Once accomplished, moving your elbow toward the outside of your body will also force your opponent's elbow to the outside of your body, weakening his lead grip.

Turning more on my right side and sitting up slightly on my right elbow, I break Dave's lead grip with my left elbow, wrap my left arm around the back of his head, and then grab his collar with my left hand.

Using my head control and legs, I pull Dave down on top of me to break his posture. At the same time, I shove his left wrist between my legs using my right hand.

I open my guard and place my left foot on Dave's right hip. In order to apply the triangle, I need to get my right leg over Dave's left shoulder.

As I push off Dave's right hip and shrimp my body toward my right, Dave realizes that I'm setting up the triangle and forces his left arm toward the outside of his body, making it difficult for me to get my right leg over his shoulder.

Instead of giving up the triangle, I utilize Dave's counter to my advantage by straightening my right arm and forcing his left arm even farther to the outside of my body. Once accomplished, I pull my right leg upward through the newly created gap.

With my right arm still locked straight to keep Dave's left arm separated from his head and body, I wrap my right leg around the left side of his head. Notice how I still have my left hand on his collar, controlling his head.

I drive Dave's upper body to my left side using my right leg. At the same time, I pull his right collar toward me using my left hand. This applies counterclockwise pressure on his head and will help me lock in the triangle.

To assume the triangle position, I hook my left leg over my right foot and then grab his right arm with my left hand. From here, I have a couple of finishing options.

Bridging my hips upward, I force Dave's right arm toward the right side of my body using my left hand. Next, I drop my hips and crunch my body forward to trap his right arm across his neck.

To finish the triangle, I squeeze my knees together, apply downward pressure with my legs, and pull Dave's head toward my chest using both of my hands.

FINISHING OPTION 2: KIMURA

In this scenario, I'm having a tough time moving Dave's right arm to the right side of my body. Instead of burning precious energy, I decide to transition into the kimura. To begin, I bend his left arm using my right hand.

Keeping my triangle position, I hook my left arm over Dave's left arm and then grab my right wrist with my left hand, establishing the kimura grip. To apply the submission, I pull my left arm toward my chest and force his left wrist in an arc toward his upper back using my right hand. With a great amount of pressure being applied to his left shoulder, he taps.

WHIZZER GRIP TO TRIANGLE

This is another way to catch your opponent in a triangle when he postures up in your guard. Just like the previous two techniques, you set up the triangle by shoving your opponent's rear hand between your legs, which clears a path to throw your leg over his shoulder. The primary difference is the control you assume upon breaking your opponent down. Instead of establishing head control, you secure a tight whizzer on his lead arm. To prevent your opponent from escaping the submission by posturing up, it is important to establish your whizzer above his elbow and lock down tight on his arm. To prevent him from escaping the submission by driving his weight forward and stacking your legs over your head, keep your foot on his hip until you've wrapped your opposite leg around the back of his head.

As Dave postures up in my guard, he establishes a right grip on my collar and a left grip along my waistline.

I grab Dave's right sleeve with my right hand and slide my left arm underneath his right arm.

I shoot my left arm upward, making sure my elbow raises past Dave's elbow. To help shatter his right grip, I pull his sleeve toward the back of my head using my right hand.

Still controlling Dave's right sleeve with my right hand, I hook my left arm tightly over his right arm and then reach my hand deep into his armpit.

Once my whizzer is wrapped tightly around Dave's right arm, I release my right sleeve grip and grab his left wrist with my right hand.

I open my guard, place my left foot on Dave's right hip, slightly shrimp my body to my left, and drive his left wrist between my legs using my right hand. Once I've trapped his left arm tight to his body, I begin swinging my right leg toward his left shoulder.

Once I've thrown my right leg over Dave's left shoulder, I release control of his left wrist and then wrap my leg around the left side of his head. To keep him from posturing up, I keep my whizzer locked tight and apply downward pressure on his head and upper back using my right leg.

Pushing off Dave's right hip with my left foot, I rotate my body in a counterclockwise direction so that my body is angled off to his side.

I hook my left leg over my right foot. Normally the next step would be to reposition his right arm to the right side of my body, but having angled my body off to his side, I can apply enough pressure to finish the submission.

COLLAR CHOKE TO TRIANGLE

Unless you're grappling with an opponent new to jiu-jitsu, chances are he will know the defense to the majority of submissions you execute from closed guard. In order to be successful, you must learn how to use your opponent's defense to transition into a second submission. The more submissions you can string together, the more likely you'll be to get one step ahead of your opponent and finish him. In this scenario, your opponent postures up in your closed guard, and you attempt to finish him with the basic collar choke demonstrated earlier in the book. Employing the most common defense, he digs his arm underneath your grip and places his hand on the side of his head, preventing you from cinching down with the choke and applying pressure to his neck. Although his defense makes it difficult to finish the choke, the positioning of his arm gives you a pathway to bring your legs up and lock in a triangle choke. The key to being successful with this technique is continuing to threaten him with the choke even as you transition into the triangle. By cinching down tight, you smash his arm into his face, obscuring his vision and making it difficult for him to see or concentrate on what you are doing with your legs. Only after assuming the triangle position do you want to release the choke.

As Dave postures up in my guard, he establishes a right grip on my collar and a left grip along my waistline. Immediately I grab his left lapel with my right hand.

I open Dave's gi using my right hand, turn toward my right side, and reach my left hand up to grab his left collar.

I slide my left fingers under Dave's left collar, hook my thumb around the outside of his collar, and then establish my grip. To stabilize my grip on his collar, I immediately pull down on his left lapel using my right hand.

I move my right hand underneath my left arm and then grab Dave's right collar.

To break Dave's posture and begin applying the choke, I pull my elbows toward the mat. Notice how this causes the blades of my wrists to dig into the sides of his neck.

As I pull my elbows toward the mat, Dave remains postured and begins sliding his left hand between my arms in defense.

Dave slides his left hand into the gap between my left arm and his face, relieving the pressure of my left wrist. Although I can still drive my right wrist into the right side of his neck, it isn't enough to finish the choke.

Although by positioning his left arm to the inside of my left arm prevents me from applying the collar choke, it allows me to easily throw my right leg over his left shoulder and transition into the triangle choke.

Using both of my legs to prevent Dave from posturing up, I release my left collar grip, place my hand on his right elbow, and push his arm toward the right side of my body.

Maintaining downward pressure with my left leg to prevent Dave from posturing up, I hook my right leg around the back of his head.

I hook the crook of my left leg over my right foot.

To finish the submission, I pinch my knees together, drive my legs downward, and pull Dave's head toward my chest using both of my hands.

AMERICANA TO TRIANGLE

In this sequence I offer another example of how to chain your submissions together from the closed guard. The technique begins by applying an Americana lock on your opponent's arm. The key is to apply the Americana as if you were trying to finish. As you drive his arm away from his body, a tremendous amount of pressure is put on his shoulder. With your opponent now focused on defending the shoulder lock, you can throw your leg over his other arm and begin locking in the triangle. However, in order to finish the triangle you still need to reposition the arm you're attacking with the Americana to the opposite side of your body. When attacking with the triangle by itself, your opponent will usually do everything in his power to prevent you from forcing his arm across his neck because he knows that it will allow you to sink in the triangle. That's not the case here. To relieve the pressure the Americana puts on his shoulder, he will most likely force his arm across his body all on his own, making your job very easy. With his arm trapped across his neck, all you have to do is pull down on his head and squeeze your legs.

As Dave attempts to posture up in my closed guard, I grab his left wrist with my right hand, wrap my left hand around the back of his neck, and pull his head downward. With his head low and his elbows bent out to the side, his posture is currently very weak.

Tired from a long battle, Dave doesn't feel like struggling against my head control and drops back down into my guard. As he does this, I maintain control of his head and left hand.

Using my right hand, I force Dave's left arm toward my left side. When his arm is within range, I feed his left wrist to my left hand and then release my right grip. Immediately I shoot my right arm up and behind his left elbow.

I wrap my right arm over Dave's left arm and then grab my left wrist with my right hand, securing a figure-four lock.

I squeeze my elbows together to secure the hold I have on Dave's left arm. At the same time, I turn toward my right side to acquire the angle I need to apply the shoulder lock.

Dave forces his left arm back toward his body to relieve pressure from his shoulder. Realizing that I can't apply enough pressure to force him to tap, I immediately begin transitioning into a triangle by throwing my left leg over his right shoulder. Although in the beginning it can be difficult to decide whether to stick with the shoulder lock or transition to the triangle, it becomes a lot easier with experience.

Applying downward pressure with my left leg to prevent Dave from posturing up, I place my right foot on his left hip, rotate my body in a clockwise direction, and use my grips to pull his arm toward my right side.

Using my left grip to keep Dave's left arm trapped to my left thigh, I release my right grip on his arm and hook my right leg over my left foot.

To finish the triangle submission, I squeeze my knees together, apply downward pressure with my legs, and pull Dave's head toward my stomach using both of my hands. It is important to note that if his head were slippery, I would grab my left shin with my right hand and pull it toward me.

HOOK TO TRIANGLE ★ BJ FAVORITE

If you have an opponent in your closed guard and he's ahead on points, he will often wrap an arm around your head, drive his weight forward, and attempt to stall his way to victory. To prevent him from accomplishing his goal you sometimes have to think outside of the box. In this sequence, I demonstrate one such technique. Instead of fighting my opponent's defensive posturing, I use it to trap one of his arms to his side. This creates a pathway to throw my leg over his arm and lock in a triangle choke.

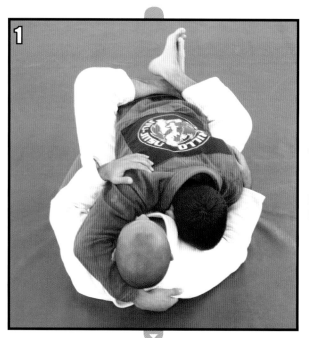

I've broken Dave down into my closed guard. Instead of fighting to posture back up, he stalls by wrapping his right arm around the back of my head. To use his positioning to my advantage, I place my left hand on his right shoulder and apply downward pressure, establish a right grip on his left triceps to help keep him broken down, and lock my legs tight to keep his weight forward.

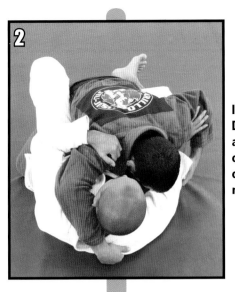

I straighten my right arm into Dave's left biceps to force his arm away from me. At the same time, I open my guard, place my left foot on the mat, and begin shrimping my hips toward my left side.

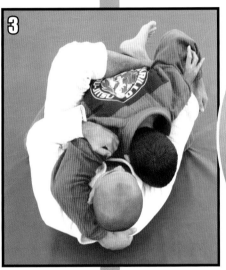

Keeping Dave's left arm pushed behind him using my right hand, I extend my left leg over his back and slide my toes underneath his arm. In order to get the necessary reach, it is important that you lead with your toes rather than your heel or the ball of your foot.

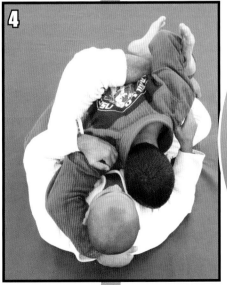

I arc my left foot so that Dave's right arm slides down the top of my foot to my instep. Once I have his arm securely trapped, I remove my right hand from his biceps.

With Dave's arm trapped to his body, I swing my right leg upward and crash it down on his left shoulder and the back of his head. At the same time, I release my left grip on his shoulder, grab the back of his right arm with my left hand, and force his elbow toward my right side. Next, I hook my right palm around the inside of his left leg. If Dave were to clamp down on my left foot with his arm to prevent me from locking in the triangle, I would yank my left foot toward my left side and toss his left leg in the same direction using my right grip, sweeping him onto his right side.

I use my right hook on Dave's left leg to rotate my body in a counterclockwise direction. As I turn, I wrap my right leg farther around the back of his head and release my hook on his left arm.

To finish the triangle, I hook the crook of my left leg over my right foot, pinch my knees together, apply downward pressure with my legs, and pull Dave's head into my abdomen using both of my hands.

TRIANGLE OFF TIGHT DEFENSE

In this sequence, your opponent prevents you from finishing the triangle by wrapping his trapped arm tightly around your leg. If you are unable to break his grip and reposition his arm across his neck, which is often necessary for finishing the triangle, a good option is to use his defense to transition into an arm bar. This is accomplished by sliding your near hand underneath his arm, positioning your opposite hand over his arm, clasping your hands together, and then using your grips to pull his arm away from your leg and up onto your shoulder. With his hand trapped to the side of your head and his arm running down the length of your chest, applying downward pressure with your arms will usually hyperextend his elbow. Your opponent will often defend by moving his arm over your head and across your body, but by doing so he allows you to accomplish your initial goal of trapping his arm across his neck. As long as you kept your legs in the triangle position, you can immediately finish the submission.

I have Dave trapped in a triangle. In order to finish the submission, I need to move his left arm to the right side of my body, but he has wrapped his left arm tightly around my right leg to prevent me from accomplishing this task.

Posturing up, Dave turns toward my left side to release pressure from the choke and escape the submission. Immediately I begin digging the fingers of my right hand underneath his left arm.

As Dave turns toward my left, I dig my right arm underneath his left arm.

I clasp my hands together above Dave's left elbow.

Using both of my arms, I roll Dave's left arm so it straightens across the length of my chest. Notice how his left hand is now pinned to the side of my neck, palm facing upward. From here, I have the option of hyperextending his left elbow by driving my arms downward.

Unable to get Dave to tap with the arm bar, I decide to transition back into the triangle. To gain better control of his left arm, I grab his elbow with my left hand and his wrist with my right hand.

Using my grips, I force Dave's left arm across his neck and to my left side.

With Dave's left arm now repositioned across his neck, I finish the triangle by pinching my knees together, applying downward pressure with my legs, and pulling his head down using both of my hands.

TRIANGLE SPRAWL OUT

As I have already mentioned, a lot of opponents are masters at defending against the triangle choke. Earlier in the book I demonstrated how to transition from the triangle into a kimura, and in the previous technique I showed how to utilize an arm lock to force your opponent's arm across his neck. In this scenario, you've managed to lock in a proper triangle, but still your opponent refuses to succumb to the submission. Instead of abandoning the choke, you post on your hands, posture up, and walk your body away from your opponent. This forces him to sprawl out on his stomach and applies even more pressure to the choke. The key to being successful with this technique is maintaining a tight triangle lock as you walk your body away. If you release the pressure for even a moment, you give your opponent an opportunity to escape.

I have Dave trapped in a triangle choke, but he is doing an excellent job resisting. To add additional pressure to the choke, I decide to transition to the triangle sprawl out. To begin, I pull my hands off the back of his head and drop my elbows to the mat.

Maintaining a tight triangle lock, I come up onto my elbows.

One by one, I graduate from my elbows to my hands, further raising my elevation and making it easier to walk my body away from Dave.

Speedily walking my body backward using my hands, Dave's body lurches forward, causing him to belly-down on the mat. To apply additional downward pressure, I crunch my body forward and drive my legs downward. With Dave's head now angled upward, there is no need to grab the back of his head with my hands to get him to tap.

TRIANGLE ARM BAR

When you capture an opponent in a triangle, a lot of the time he will attempt to release pressure from his neck by pulling his head upward. Although this defense makes it difficult to finish the triangle, it allows you to make an easy transition into the triangle arm bar. With his head elevated, all you have to do is throw a leg over his head, pin his trapped arm to your chest, and then finish the new submission by bridging your hips.

I have Dave trapped in a triangle choke, but he is defending by pulling his head upward. Instead of burning out my legs holding on to the triangle, I decide to make a quick transition into a triangle arm bar. To begin, I hook my right arm over his right wrist to pin his arm to my chest.

I use Dave's upward pressure to my advantage by hooking my left leg over the left side of his head, trapping his right arm between my legs. In order to be successful with this step, you must reposition your leg before your opponent can apply downward pressure, which is the most common counter to the triangle arm bar. Notice how I cross my left leg over my right leg. Not only does this position his head and arm directly between my legs, but it will also help prevent my left leg from sliding off the top of his head as I apply downward pressure.

To finish the submission, I keep Dave's right arm trapped to my chest, apply downward pressure with my legs, and bridge my hips into his elbow.

TRIANGLE TO ARM BAR TO TRIANGLE

In this sequence, your opponent attempts to relieve pressure from his neck and escape the triangle by standing and pulling his head upward. To capitalize on his defense, hook his leg with your arm and then use that hook to turn your body perpendicular to his. With his captured arm now lined up in the center of your chest, you transition to the triangle arm bar, just as you did in the previous technique. Immediately your opponent's defense strategy will change. Posturing up will no longer help him. In order to escape the triangle arm bar, he will most likely drop down to his knees and drive his weight into you. Although this makes it difficult to finish the triangle arm bar, it creates a perfect scenario to transition back to the triangle. The reason this combination works so well is because the defenses for the two submissions are the opposite of each other. By attempting to escape the triangle, he straightens his arm and allows you to transition into the triangle arm bar. Next, he attempts to escape the triangle arm bar by getting his head closer to you, making for an easy transition back into the triangle. Becoming a master at flowing back and forth between these two techniques will dramatically increases your effectiveness from the guard. The most important thing to focus on is the angle of your body. When you move into the triangle arm bar, it is important to turn your body perpendicular to your opponent so you gain proper leverage on his arm.

I've caught Dave in a triangle and I'm working to finish the submission.

Dave stands up and pulls his head upward. This relieves slight pressure from his neck, provides him with leverage, and gives him several options to escape the submission. Immediately I release control of his head and grab his right wrist with my left hand.

I hook my right arm around the inside of Dave's left leg and then use that as an anchor to rotate my body in a counterclockwise direction. Although it's possible to finish the triangle from this new angle, I don't want to take any chances and continue to make my transition.

Instead of holding on to the triangle, I quickly hook my left leg around the left side of Dave's head to trap his arm between my legs. Although this transition is a gamble, your success rate will rise significantly as long as you move quickly and angle your body off to the side. It is important to notice that I've hooked my left leg on top of my right to prevent my left leg from sliding off his forehead.

Having used Dave's defense for the triangle to capture him in an arm bar, he realizes his mistake and drops his weight onto my legs to bend his trapped arm and escape the submission.

As Dave drops his weight over my legs and clasps his hands together, I realize that it will be difficult to finish the arm bar. However, by defending against the arm bar he has once again made himself vulnerable to the triangle. To begin the transition, I use my left hand to keep his right arm to my right side, pull him downward using my legs, and slide my left leg toward the right side of his head. Notice how I have kept my feet hooked together for a smooth transition.

As Dave collapses into my guard, I hook the crook of my left leg over my right foot, squeeze my knees together, apply downward pressure with my legs, and pull his head toward my stomach using both of my hands.

SHOULDER LOCK OPTION OFF TRIANGLE

When you capture your opponent in a triangle choke, you trap his head and one of his arms. Finishing him with the triangle submission is the most obvious option, but if his triangle defense is sharp, it is important to remember that you can also attack his wrist, elbow, or shoulder. In this sequence, you focus on your opponent's shoulder. This is accomplished by positioning his elbow on one side of his body, and then forcing his wrist to the other. It is a very powerful and quick submission.

I've caught Dave in the triangle position. In order to finish the submission, I need to reposition his arm to my right side.

I grab Dave's right wrist with my right hand and force his arm toward the right side of my body. To help aid this push, I also use my left hand. In this scenario, I am able to move his right elbow past my centerline and off to my right side. Although I still have the triangle locked in, I decide to use the positioning of his right elbow to apply a shoulder lock. To begin, I thrust my hips upward to trap his elbow to my right side.

Using both of my hands, I force Dave's wrist toward my left side. With his right elbow trapped to my right side, his arm bends unnaturally, putting a tremendous amount of pressure on his right shoulder. With Dave currently losing consciousness from the triangle choke, it is difficult for him to defend against this second submission.

WRIST LOCK OFF TRIANGLE

When you lock in a triangle, you separate one of your opponent's arms from his core, allowing you to attack it with a number of different submissions. In this sequence, you apply a wrist lock. For the best results, it is important to line up your opponent's elbow with the center your chest before locking in the submission. This will provide a backstop and ensure that you have the leverage needed to apply proper pressure on his wrist. If his elbow slides off to one side of your body or the other, it's still possible to finish, but it becomes less likely. When utilizing this technique, you must be careful. A lot of jiu-jitsu practitioners are accustomed to getting their arms hyperextended and, as a result, know when to submit. Wrist locks are not employed nearly as often, so it's possible to injure your opponent before he realizes it's in his best interest to tap.

With Dave caught in the triangle position, I'm using both of my hands to pull his right arm toward the right side of my body.

Using my right grip on Dave's right wrist, I pull his hand to my right side. To help with this task, I push on his right elbow using my left hand. Once accomplished, I use my right hand to turn his right palm upward.

I wrap my left arm over Dave's right arm. Next, I grab my right wrist with my left hand, securing a figure-four lock.

To apply the wrist lock, I reposition Dave's arm so it is running down my centerline. Next, I use my lock to drive the fingers of his right hand toward his right wrist. It is important to notice that I've kept my elbows tight to my body to increase pressure. If you let your elbows drift out to the sides, it gives your opponent an opportunity to pull his trapped arm free.

TRIANGLE TO MOUNT TRANSITION ★ BJ FAVORITE

A lot of jiu-jitsu practitioners will panic and do irrational things when you capture them in a triangle. In an attempt to escape the choke, they'll sometimes stand up prior to posturing, which positions their head in front of their body. Instead of just focusing on the submission, a good option is to use the forward positioning of his head to force him into a forward roll. By rolling with him, you'll end up in the mounted triangle position. To be effective with this technique, it is important to move your head to the side as you roll so as not to injure your neck. It is also important to keep the triangle locked tight. If you lose your opponent's head during the roll, he'll not only escape the submission, but he'll also have an opportunity to take your back.

I've caught Dave in a very tight triangle. To counter, he grabs his right wrist with his left hand and manages to relieve enough pressure to avoid tapping.

Dave posts his left foot on the mat to relieve slight pressure from his neck.

Dave stands to relieve more pressure from his neck and increase his escape options. Keeping a tight lock with my legs, my hips get pulled off the mat.

As my hips increase in elevation, I angle my head toward my left side just like I would when executing a forward roll, post my left hand on the mat with a base grip, and push my shoulders toward Dave's legs. At the same time, I pull Dave's head downward using my right hand, causing him to lose balance and fall forward.

As I continue to push off with my left hand, drive my legs toward the mat, and pull down on Dave's head, he loses his balance completely, causing his head to drop to the mat. Although he posts his left hand to hinder his roll, I'm applying enough downward pressure to shatter his post.

As I drive my legs to the mat, I use my posted left hand to elevate my head. Notice how I have kept the triangle locked tight.

Still pushing off my left hand, I sit up and force Dave to collapse to his back. With a mounted triangle already locked in, I finish the submission by squeezing my knees together, applying pressure to the back of his head using my legs, and pulling his head upward using both of my hands.

TRIANGLE DEFENSE TO SINGLE LEG

In the previous sequence you caught your opponent in a triangle and he panicked. Instead of utilizing proper technique, he hastily stood up before posturing, allowing you to roll him over to his back and claim the mount position. Although it's great when you can threaten your opponent to the point where he makes a crucial mistake, a lot of opponents will maintain their cool when caught in a fight-ending submission. In this sequence, you have a triangle locked tight, but your opponent stays sharp and postures prior to standing. Once he has released pressure from his neck and broken your triangle lock, attempting to hold on to the submission will often allow him to obtain an advantageous position. Rather than waiting for that to happen, you abandon the triangle, flip backward onto all fours, shoot in for a single leg, and haul your opponent to his back. A part of what makes this technique so effective is that it's unorthodox. Techniques become orthodox because they are effective, but the downside is that most competitors know the counters. Unorthodox techniques can also be effective, but they have the added bonus of being able to catch your opponent off guard.

Caught in a triangle, Dave postures up to relieve pressure from his neck.

With a mission to stand to increase his escape options, Dave posts his left foot on the mat. This is the point where I must decide to either keep his head down or allow him to increase his elevation. In this case, I decide to permit him to stand.

As Dave stands up, I keep my feet locked together and relax my legs, causing my body to elongate. To prepare for my attack and protect my neck, I post my left hand and right elbow on the mat.

Still maintaining a tight lock on Dave's head, I cock my neck backward toward his legs. From here, I will drop down to my knees, but it is important to align your head before making your move. If you go too soon and have to readjust the positioning of your head, your opponent will have a greater ability to drop down on top of you and take your back.

Supporting my weight on my left hand and right elbow, I release my head control by unhooking my feet.

I drop my left foot to the mat and begin elevating my head using my arms.

As I drop down to my knees, I immediately wrap my left hand around Dave's right ankle and drive my left shoulder into his right knee. By pulling his ankle toward me and plowing my shoulder into his knee, I slightly hyperextend his leg and make it very difficult for him to defend against the single-leg takedown.

TRIANGLE POSITION FINISHES

As Dave collapses, he posts his right hand on the mat to help him stand back up. To prevent him from accomplishing his goal, I maintain control of his right leg using my left arm.

Continuing to drive my weight forward, I flatten Dave out on the mat. Immediately I reach my right arm forward and grab his left leg to prevent him from scrambling.

I drive my right knee between Dave's legs, post my right foot on the mat, and posture up. From here, I will work to pass his open guard.

ARM ATTACKS

ARM ATTACKS

In this section I cover the arm attacks that are available from the closed guard. As you will see, there are numerous submission that you can employ. You can attack your opponent's wrist with a wristlock. You can attack his elbow with a straight or inverted arm bar. You an also attack his shoulder by transitioning into a kimura, Americana, or omoplata. However, in order to be successful with any of these submissions, you must gain control of your opponent's entire arm. For example, in order to properly secure a wristlock, you must not only secure your opponent's wrist, but also his elbow and shoulder. To successfully attack his elbow with a straight arm lock, you need to control his wrist and shoulder. And in order to apply a shoulder lock, you must capture his wrist and elbow. If you fail to obtain complete control of your opponent's arm from his wrist up to his shoulder, the techniques in this section will be very difficult to execute. For this reason, it is imperative that you study each step carefully and set up the submissions properly.

STRAIGHT ARM BARS

The straight arm bar is one of the most effective submissions from the closed guard. However, in order to be successful with the technique, there are a few steps that must be followed. For starters, you must isolate one of your opponent's arms. If he has his arms tucked tight to his body, this can sometimes be difficult to manage. To get around this blockade, trap the arm you want to attack to your chest using both of your hands. Next, maneuver your hips underneath his elbow to further isolate his arm. As long as you're controlling his entire arm—meaning his wrist, elbow, and shoulder—you can hyperextend his elbow by throwing your leg over his head and bridging your hips upward. It is important to note that when executing arm bars wrist control is very important. You want to secure your opponent's wrist so that his thumb is pointing in the opposite direction of his elbow. If you fail to assume this position prior to applying the arm bar, the submission will not work.

Although the arm bar submission is rather straightforward, there are a number of ways to set it up from the closed guard. You can apply the submission when your opponent is kneeing in your guard, when he is posting on one foot, or when he stands up on both feet. In the coming section, I demonstrate how to catch your opponent with the arm bar from each of these positions, but it is important to remember that you won't always be successful with your initial attack. In order to increase your chances of locking in a finishing hold, I've also included your opponent's most common defenses to the arm bar, and how to use those defenses to transition into other submissions. I recommend practicing these transitions as much as possible because they allow you to get one step ahead of your opponent. If you are slow to capitalize on your opponent's reactions, you allow him to regroup and strengthen his defenses.

SHOULDER LOCKS

In this section I cover the kimura and Americana shoulder lock submissions. Although shoulder locks are often more difficult to finish than straight arm bars, the locks offer an excellent form of control. Even if you are unable to force your opponent to tap by cranking on his shoulder, he will be forced to defend against the submission and most likely stall in the position, creating an opportunity for you execute other attacks such as sweeps, straight arm bars, omoplatas, and triangles. However, the only way to get him to defend is to threaten him with the shoulder lock, which means you must commit to the submission. If you transition to a secondary submission too soon, you'll not only miss out on a possible shoulder lock, but you'll also miss out on an opportunity to capitalize on your opponent's defense.

OMOPLATA SETUPS

In this section I demonstrate a number of ways to establish the omoplata position from the closed guard, which is the first step to securing the omoplata submission. At the end of the first technique, I show the standard shoulder lock finish. Although ideal, it's one of the more difficult submissions to pull off because your opponent has more defenses than with most submissions. However, you can use these defenses to transition to other attacks, such as wrist locks, straight arm locks, foot locks, and sweeps. Due to the importance of learning how to properly set up the omoplata position, as well as the number of alternate finishes based upon your opponent's defense, I have dedicated two sections to the omoplata. It is important to study this section first because without the ability to reach the omoplata position and threaten your opponent with the shoulder lock, you won't be able to utilize all of your various options. Only after you have thoroughly practiced the setups and the basic omoplata should you tackle the submissions that stem off the shoulder lock.

SUBMISSIONS FROM OMOPLATA CONTROL

As I already mentioned, finishing your opponent with the omoplata shoulder lock is often difficult. This is primarily due to positioning. When you secure the omoplata position, the majority of the time your opponent will be on all fours, which means he still has a strong base. As you attempt to lock in the omoplata, he can use that base to posture up or execute a forward roll, two common escapes. Luckily, there are several answers for both scenarios. If your opponent attempts to posture up and shatter your control, apply downward pressure to the back of his shoulder using your leg. Keeping his posture broken in this manner and completing the omoplata submission can be difficult, but you have several other options. As you will soon see, with your opponent's arm trapped between your legs, you can attack his wrist, elbow, or foot. If your opponent should attempt to escape the omoplata submission by executing a for-

ward roll, you also have several options. You can turn his escape into a sweep and obtain top control, or you can transition into a submission such as an arm bar or knee bar. When you're armed with all of these options, it puts your opponent between a rock and a hard place. No matter which way he moves to escape the omoplata, you have an answer. However, it is critical to have a stealthy omoplata. If you fail to threaten your opponent with the shoulder lock, you won't have the opportunity to capitalize on his escape.

STANDARD ARM BAR

The standard arm bar is one of the most utilized submission from the guard, from white belts to black belts. It's an important technique to master not just because it's an effective submission, but also because there are numerous options that stem off of it. The key to being successful with this move is obtaining tight control over your opponent's arm, posting your foot on his hip, and shifting your body off line from his body to acquire the angle needed to attack his arm. It's also important to keep your opponent super tight and position his arm straight down the center of your chest, which gives you the leverage needed to hyperextend his elbow. It's not a high percentage technique because most jiu-jitsu practitioners are familiar with the submission. But as you will see in the coming section, there are numerous ways to take advantage of your opponent's counters.

As Dave postures up in my guard, he establishes a right grip on my collar and a left grip along my waistline.

I establish a strong right grip on Dave's left sleeve. At the same time, I reach my left hand underneath his right arm.

I cup my left hand over Dave's left elbow.

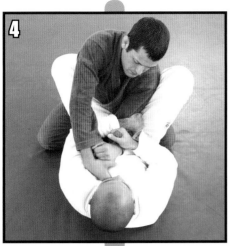

Controlling just above Dave's left elbow, I force his left arm to bend downward toward my stomach using my left hand. At the same time, I open my guard, place my right foot on his left hip, and break his left grip by pulling his sleeve toward my head using my right hand.

Pushing off Dave's left hip using my right foot, I rotate my body in a clockwise direction. At the same time, I hook my left arm over his left arm to secure it tightly to my chest, release my right grip on his sleeve, and hook my left leg over his upper back. To prevent him from posturing up, I apply downward pressure with my left leg. It is important to mention that if I were to remove my right foot from his left hip, he could once again square his body up with mine and eliminate the angle I need to secure the arm bar.

I drive Dave's head toward my right side using my right hand. This will prevent him from squaring his hips with mine as I remove my right foot from his hip.

I wrap my right leg around the right side of Dave's head. To apply the submission, I keep his left arm trapped to my chest, pinch my knees together, apply downward pressure with my legs, and bridge my hips. With his elbow hyperextended, he taps.

ARM BAR TO TRIANGLE

In this sequence you apply the standard arm bar just as you did in the last, but your opponent counters by driving his upper body into you and pulling his trapped arm away from you. Although it's important not to give up on submissions to quickly, it's also very important not to hang on to them for too long. If his elbow slips past your groin, you no longer have the leverage needed to hyperextend his arm. In such a case, you want to immediately abandon the arm bar and transition into a triangle. With your opponent driving his upper body forward and his trapped arm away, he does most of the work for you. All you have to do is reposition your legs and lock in the triangle. In order to be effective with this technique, you must learn how to feel your opponent's movements with your body. If you allow him pull his trapped arm entirely free and post his hand on the mat, his options become many. For the best results, make the transition the instant you lose his elbow.

I've forced Dave's left arm to bend downward using my left hand, opened my guard, placed my right foot on his left hip, and broken his left grip by pulling his sleeve toward my head using my right hand.

Pushing off Dave's left hip with my right foot, I rotate my body in a clockwise direction.

With my left arm wrapped tightly over Dave's left arm, I push his head away from me using my right hand. Next, I wrap my right leg around the right side of his head.

Before I can bridge my hips and hyperextend Dave's right elbow, he pulls his left elbow out from between my legs. In order to capture him in a triangle, I must make my transition before he frees his left arm completely and posts his hand on the mat.

I was too slow. Before I could wrap my right leg over Dave's left shoulder, he pulled his left arm free and posted his hand on the mat, giving him the leverage to stand up. From this position, it will be very difficult for me to capture him in a triangle.

I beat Dave's escape by rotating in a counterclockwise direction and hooking my right leg over his left shoulder before he can post his hand on the mat. To prevent him from posturing up, I apply downward pressure with my legs.

I grab Dave's right sleeve with my right hand and his right elbow with my left hand. Next, I force his right arm toward my right side using my grips and drive my right leg into the left side of his head.

Hooking the crook of my left leg over my right foot, I apply downward pressure and release my right grip on his sleeve.

To finish the submission, I pinch my knees together, apply downward pressure using my legs, and pull Dave's head toward my stomach using both of my hands.

PLATFORM ARM BAR

The primary difference between this technique and the standard arm bar is the amount of control you gain over your opponent's arm. In addition to grabbing your opponent's sleeve, you also establish a cross grip above his elbow, making it very difficult for him to pull his arm away from you as you put your foot on his hip and angle your body off to the side. Although the technique requires you to release your cross grip before applying the submission, you do not want to let it go too early. Only after you have assumed the arm bar position and broken his base by driving your leg into his side should you change your grips. If you let go too early, your opponent will have an opportunity to escape. It's important to learn and practice the standard arm bar, but when up against a strong or experienced opponent, the platform arm bar is often a good substitution. You can never have too much control.

As Dave postures up in my guard, he establishes a right grip on my collar and a left grip along my waistline. To setup my attack, I move my right hand toward his left sleeve.

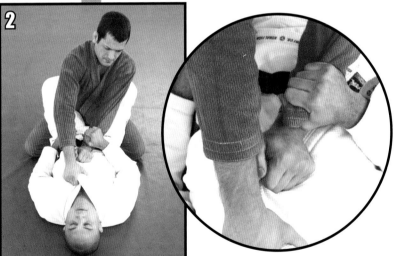

I establish a powerful grip on Dave's left sleeve. Notice how I have bunched the fabric in my hand and then closed my fist tight. Once accomplished, I tuck my right elbow tight to my side and pull his arm toward's me.

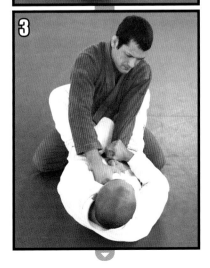

I reach my left arm underneath Dave's right arm and then grip the seam of his gi above his left elbow. Grabbing the seams of your opponent's uniform gives you the most control. For the best results, you want to place your fingers on one side of the seam, your palm on the other, and close your hand tight. To create a platform behind Dave's elbow, I drive my palm upward into his arm.

I pull Dave's left arm toward me using both of my grips, causing him to lean forward.

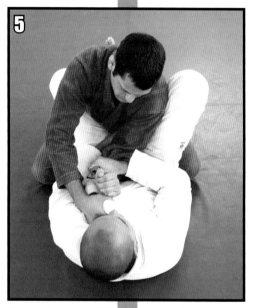

Continuing to pull Dave's trapped arm toward me, I open my guard and place my right foot on his hip. To make a smooth transition into the arm bar, I keep my left leg elevated and relaxed.

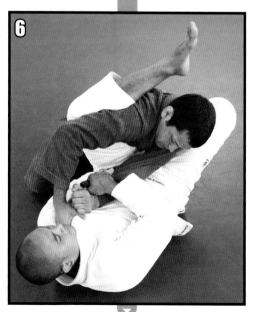

Driving off Dave's left hip with my right foot, I angle my body off to the side. At the same time, I drive into his right side with my left leg and straighten his left arm across my chest using my right grip.

Having assumed the arm bar position, I release my left grip on Dave's elbow and wrap my left arm over his left arm.

I slide my left arm up to Dave's wrist to keep his arm pinned to my chest. Next, I release my right grip and place my hand on the side of his head. To disrupt his base and create the space I need to apply the arm bar, I drive him away from me using my left leg and right hand.

I swing my right leg over Dave's head. To hyperextend his elbow and finish the arm bar, I keep his left arm pinned to my chest, drive my legs into him, and bridge my hips.

COLLAR GRIP ARM BAR

In this sequence, you setup the arm bar by grabbing above your opponent's elbow with one hand and establishing a cross collar grip with the other. Latching on to your opponent's collar has several benefits—it makes it difficult for him to posture up and avoid the arm bar, and it will often trick him into thinking you're attempting to apply a choke. Once you have your grips, you move into the arm bar position just as you did with the platform arm bar, but since you're attached to his upper body with your collar choke, it becomes much more difficult for him to pull his trapped arm free and escape. Just as with the platform arm bar, after collapsing your opponent's base, throw your leg over his head, reposition your grips, and apply the submission.

As Dave postures up in my guard, he establishes a left grip on my collar and a right grip along my waistline.

I grab the seam of Dave's left sleeve above his elbow using my right hand and reach my left hand up to establish a basic collar grip. The fingers of my left hand are inside his collar, my thumb is on the outside, and my palm is facing his left shoulder. Notice how I have turned slightly onto my right side to increase the reach of my left arm.

I place my right foot on Dave's left hip.

Driving off Dave's left hip with my right foot, I angle my body away from his lead grip. This is important; you always want to rotate away from your opponent's lead grip rather than toward it. At that same, I pull on his left collar using my left hand and slide my left leg up to his right shoulder and apply downward pressure. Having straightened his left arm using my elbow control, my rotation and downward pressure collapses his base.

Having assumed the arm bar position, I release my left grip on Dave's collar and slide my left forearm over his left wrist to keep his arm pinned to his chest.

I release my right grip on Dave's left elbow, place my right hand on the side of his head, and then force him away from me to further disrupt his base and create the space I need to swing my leg over his head.

I swing my right leg over Dave's head. To finish the arm bar, I keep his left arm pinned to my chest, drive into him using my legs, and bridge my hips. The combination of these actions hyperextends his elbow, forcing him to tap.

STRAIGHT ARM BARS

OPPONENT KNEELING

SHOULDER CONTROL ARM BAR

In this technique you don't attack your opponent's straight arm grips or disrupt his base. All you do is angle your body off to the side so you can throw your leg over his shoulder to trap it. The important part of this technique are your grips. If you're attacking your opponent's left arm, you want to grab above his left elbow with one hand and establish a cross collar grip with the other to prevent him from pulling his arm away from you as you maneuver your leg over his shoulder. Once accomplished, you have several finishing options. You can apply the arm bar with your leg still over his shoulder or you can transition to the standard finish by throwing your leg over his head. And as with the other arm bar techniques shown in this section, if he should manage to pull his trapped arm free and escape from the arm bar, you can use his defense to apply the triangle.

As Dave postures up in my guard, he establishes a right grip on my collar and a left grip along my waistline.

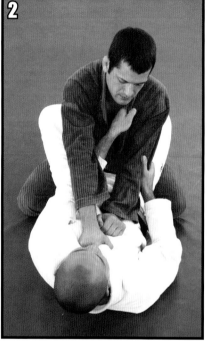

I grip the seam of Dave's left sleeve above his elbow using my right hand. At the same time, I reach my left arm underneath his right arm and grab his left collar. The collar grip doesn't have to be too deep; the important part is that you double up on the left side of your opponent's body. If he has his right arm back, you'll want to double up on his right side.

As I open my guard, I maintain both of my grips. If I were to lose control of Dave's left side, he would be able to use his left elbow and left knee to further open my guard and pass to my right side.

Maintaining both of my grips, I clamp my right leg down over his left shoulder and then cross my left foot over my right. If needed, you can push off your opponents shoulder using your right leg to rotate your body to the left and acquire the proper angle to finish the arm bar.

Having assumed the angled I need to finish the arm bar, I swing my right leg over Dave's head.

I release my left grip on Dave's collar, wrap my left hand over my right to pin his arm to my chest, curl my legs downward, and bridge my hips. As Dave's elbow becomes hyperextended, he has no choice but to tap.

BASE CONTROL ARM BAR

In order to gain the leverage needed to apply an arm bar from guard, you must angle your body off to the side. If your opponent is a master at preventing you from acquiring this dominant angle, this is an excellent technique to employ. As with several of the previous techniques, you begin by latching on to the arm you want to attack above the elbow. However, instead of securing a cross collar grip with your opposite hand, you secure an inside knee grip. To acquire the proper angle, all you have to do is pull your body toward his knee using your grip. Again, you're not directly attacking your opponent straight arm grips, but rather attacking them indirectly, which can dramatically increase your chance of success. The most important part of the technique is to maintain both of your grips. If you lose either, abort mission and return to closed guard.

As Dave postures up in my guard, he establishes a right grip on my collar and a left grip along my waistline. Immediately I grab the seam of his right sleeve above his elbow.

Pulling on Dave's right arm using my left hand to disrupt his base, I grab the inside of his left pant leg using my right hand. It is important to notice that my right thumb is pointing toward his knee and my right elbow is turned into my body. Using this grip and my left foot, I rotate my body in a counterclockwise direction. At the same time, I relax my right leg and begin wrapping it around his left side. It is important to note that with my right grip I can also punch his left knee away from me to further disrupt his base.

Continuing to rotate my body in a counterclockwise direction to disrupt Dave's base and assume the angle I need to attack his arm, I apply a little downward pressure on his left shoulder using my right leg and swing my left leg toward the left side of his head. Notice how I'm using my left grip on his right sleeve to pull on his arm and disrupt his base.

As I swing my left leg toward the left side of Dave's head, I drive my right leg into his side, elevate his left leg off the mat using my right hand, and pull his right arm into me using my left hand. The combination of these actions shatters his base and causes him to collapse to his right.

As Dave attempts to drive his left knee to the ground to reacquire his base, I swing my left leg over his head. Having distracted him with the sweep, he has totally forgotten about the vulnerability of his right arm. With my left grip on his right sleeve intact, I will now transition into the arm bar.

To prevent Dave from countering, I utilize a quick arm bar finish by sliding the crook of my left arm up to his right wrist to trap his arm to my chest, applying downward pressure with my legs, and bridging my hips upward to hyperextend his elbow.

FORWARD BASE ARM BAR

The majority of jiu-jitsu practitioners train to face other people who also know jiu-jitsu. As a result, they often don't learn how to capitalize on mistakes that jiu-jitsu practitioners are taught to avoid. In this sequence, your opponent secures two collar grips and drives his weight forward in your guard to apply a collar choke. This is highly frowned upon in traditional jiu-jitsu, but it happens quite often in the lower belts or when you're up against an unorthodox player. To use his attack to your advantage, you establish a grip on his sleeve to ensure his commitment to the choke and then reach your opposite hand between his legs, which allows you to turn your body and acquire the angle needed to attack his arm. The key to being successful with this technique is drilling so often that it becomes a reaction. When your opponent leans forward for the choke, the majority of the time he will quickly realize his vulnerability and abandon the position, so you must capitalize quickly.

As Dave postures up in my guard, he establishes a right grip on my collar and a left grip along my waistline. Immediately I reach my hands over his arms and grab his sleeves.

Using my grips, I pull Dave into me. Thinking he is being slick, he grabs my collar with his left hand and then goes with my energy in an attempt to apply a forward choke and stand up.

Dave punches his right hand into the choke, giving him a base that he can use to stand.

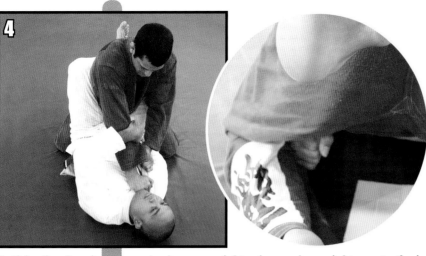

Anticipating Dave's actions, I release my right grip, reach my right arm to the inside of his left leg, tighten my right hand in a fist, and then hook the back of my fist around the back of his knee.

Keeping my right leg relaxed, I use my hook to pull my body in a counterclockwise angle and swing my left leg toward the left side of Dave's head.

I continue to use my right hook on Dave's left leg to rotate my body in a counterclockwise direction. Once my body is perpendicular to his, I hook my left leg around the left side of his head. It is important to mention that timing is very important in this technique. Notice how I don't have an elaborate grip on my opponent's right arm. I can get away with this because I transition into the arm bar while he is still driving his arms down into me. If your timing is off, it will be very easy for your opponent to pull his arm free and avoid the submission.

To apply a quick arm bar finish, I slide the crook of my left arm up to Dave's wrist to trap his arm to my chest, apply downward pressure with my legs, and bridge my hips upward to hyperextend his elbow.

COLLAR CHOKE TO ARM BAR

If your opponent has tight defense, it can difficult to finish him with a single attack, making it important to have a large number of combinations in your arsenal. In this scenario, you apply the collar choke demonstrated earlier in the book, but are unable to break his posture and finish. Instead of giving up on the submission, you use it as a distraction as you move your body off to his side and acquire the angle needed to attack his arm. Once accomplished, you have several submissions at your disposal. You can continue with the choke, apply the arm bar, or transition to the triangle should he pull his arm free. When you throw a single attack at your opponent, you give him a problem to solve. When you string your attacks together, you present a crisis. The key to being successful with this technique is making the choke believable and holding on to it until you are ready to switch to the arm bar. If you let go too soon, the crisis you presented once again becomes just a problem.

As Dave postures up in my guard, he establishes a right grip on my collar and a left grip along my waistline.

Turning onto my right side, I grab Dave's left collar with my right hand and open it.

I slide the fingers of my left hand into Dave's left collar, establishing a tight collar grip.

I slide my right arm underneath my left arm and then grab Dave's right collar with my right hand. Notice how both of my thumbs are on the outside of his collar and my palms are facing away from his head. This will allow me to drive the blades of my forearms into the sides of his neck. It is also important to notice that my head is angled slightly to my right side to apply a more powerful choke.

Dave maintains his posture, making it difficult for me to lock in a tight choke. Instead of burning all of my energy trying to finish, I use my positioning to transition into my second attack. To accomplish this, I place my left foot on his right hip and then use it as an anchor to rotate my body in a counterclockwise direction.

Maintaining pressure with the choke, I move my right leg up to Dave's left armpit. Now that I have assumed the arm bar position, I will apply the submission.

Applying downward pressure to Dave's left shoulder using my right leg, I swing my left leg toward the left side of his head. Notice that I still have not released the choke.

Hooking my left leg around the left side of Dave's head, I release my left grip on his collar and slide the crook of my left arm over his right wrist to trap his arm to my chest. To finish the submission, I apply downward pressure with my legs and bridge my hips.

GI TRAP ARM BAR

If your opponent is a master at grip fighting, it can sometimes be difficult to gain control of the arm you want to attack. Although the gi trap arm bar is somewhat flashy, it's highly effective because instead of directly grabbing your opponent's sleeve, you wrap up his arm with the lapel of his own gi, leading to much stronger control. By pulling tight on his lapel as you angle your body off to the side, you hyperextend his arm and shatter his grip. This causes his base to collapse and allows you to transition into the arm bar. The keys to success are wrapping his gi above his elbow and continuing to pull on his arm until his base is broken and you're ready to throw your leg over his head.

As Dave postures up in my guard, he establishes a right grip on my collar and a left grip along my waistline.

I reach my left hand underneath Dave's right arm and grab his left lapel.

I reach my right hand underneath Dave's left arm. Next, I pass his left lapel from my left hand to my right hand. When executing this step, it helps to be sneaky. By directing your eyes toward your left side, you can steal your opponent's focus away from what you are doing with your right hand. This might seem insignificant, but it works better than you'd think.

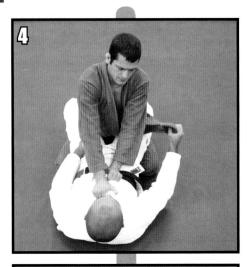

I pull Dave's lapel toward my right side.

I quickly pull Dave's left lapel over his arm above his elbow. Next, I reach my left hand underneath my right hand to re-grab his sleeve. It is important to notice that my left palm is facing away from me, allowing me to quickly establish a grip. If you don't act quickly, your opponent will most likely pull his arm free.

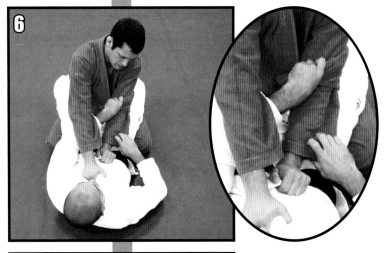

Once I establish my left grip on Dave's left lapel, I pull it as tight as possible around his biceps, trapping his arm.

Continuing to pull on Dave's lapel using my left hand, I grab his left sleeve with my right hand to help force his arm toward my left side.

I place my right foot on Dave's left hip, and then use it as an anchor to rotate my body in a clockwise direction. At the same time, I place my left leg over his right shoulder and apply outward pressure. Since I have his left arm trapped, he is unable to post his hand and maintain his base. It is important to notice that his left arm is currently running down the center of my chest.

With Dave's base broken, I release my right grip on his sleeve and force his head away from me using my right hand. Notice how I am still pulling on his left lapel using my left hand.

I throw my right leg over Dave's head. To finish the arm bar, I apply downward pressure with my legs, secure his arm to my chest using both of my hands, and bridge my hips.

GRIP TEASE ARM BAR

When you're having trouble launching an attack from closed guard, it can sometimes be beneficial to bait your opponent. There are many guard-opening techniques that require sleeve control, so a lot of the time he will go for your arm. Instead of yanking your arm away as he makes his move, pull it away just fast enough to avoid his grip. As long as you keep your arm within his reach, he will often chase it, causing him to extend himself forward. When his posture is broke and his arm straight, let him grab your sleeve. Before he can use the grip to his advantage, wrap up his arm with your opposite hand to secure it to your chest, angle your body off to the side, and apply the arm bar. The key to success is properly baiting your opponent. It's a lot like fishing—if you jerk the bait away too quickly, he'll sense danger and move on to something else. If you dangle it in front of him and then slowly pull it away, his mind will become fixated on having his prize.

As Dave postures up in my guard, he establishes a right grip on my collar. Instead of securing a left grip along my waistline, he eyes my right sleeve. If I allow him to establish the grip, he could use it to help stand up and open my guard.

I elevate my right arm to entice Dave into going for my sleeve. As he reaches his for it, I begin pulling my right arm toward the back of my head. It is important not to pull away too quickly. In order for the bait to work, you must keep your arm within grabbing distance.

I pull my right arm behind my head. Having pulled it away slowly enough for Dave to become fixated on it, he continues to reach for it by leaning forward. As he breaks his posture, I reach my left arm toward his right arm.

Dave leans all the way forward to establish a grip on my right sleeve. To capitalize on his mistake, I hook my left hand over his left arm above his elbow, open my guard, and place my right foot on his left hip.

Pushing off Dave's left hip with my right foot, I rotate my body in a clockwise direction. Notice how I move my right arm toward my left side. With Dave still grabbing my right sleeve, this action repositions his arm down the length of my chest, allowing me to apply the arm bar. At the same time, I hook my left leg over his back and begin applying downward pressure on his upper body.

Having assumed the arm bar position, I break Dave's grip on my right sleeve. To further disrupt his base and create the space I need to throw my leg over his head, I drive his head away from me using my right forearm.

I throw my right leg over Dave's head, slide my left arm up to his left wrist, and grab the crook of his left arm with my right hand. To finish the submission, I apply downward pressure with my legs, keep his left arm trapped to my chest, and bridge my hips.

OCTOPUS GUARD TO ARM BAR ★ BJ FAVORITE

In the majority of jiu-jitsu academies, practitioners learn the same basic moves and how to defend against them. If your opponent is the same skill level, he will often be able to shut down your traditional offense. To catch him off guard, sometimes your best bet is to pull out a nontraditional technique, such as the one demonstrated in the sequence below. It's set up a little differently than the previous arm bars in that you latch on to the sleeve of your opponent's rear post with both hands, and then use that control to break his grip and pull his arm up and across your body. This puts your opponent in an awkward position—his body is now angled off to your side, and his rear post is lying across your torso. To prevent him from turning back into you and squaring his hips, you clamp down on the arm draped across your torso with a tight whizzer. This places you in the octopus guard and gives you several options. The first option is to take your opponent's back, which is what I did when I fought Matt Hughes for the second time in the UFC. However, taking your opponent's back requires leverage you don't always have, and even when you do have it, the transition demands a good deal of exertion. A lot of times the better option is to apply an arm bar directly from the octopus guard.

As Dave postures up in my guard, he establishes a right grip on my collar and a left grip along my waistline. To set up my attack, I grab his right wrist with my left hand and grab the cuff of his left sleeve with my right hand.

Once I've established a solid grip on Dave's left sleeve with my right hand, I reach my left arm over his right arm and establish a second grip on his left sleeve.

Jerking both of my hands toward my head, I break Dave's left grip along my waistline.

Releasing my left grip on Dave's right sleeve, I turn onto my right side and shoot my left arm underneath his right arm. At the same time, I use my right grip on his sleeve to pull his arm behind my head. It is important to notice that my left elbow is lined up with his left elbow. If your arm is below your opponent's elbow, you will be unable to properly trap his arm.

Falling toward my back, I wrap my left arm over the back of Dave's left arm, collapsing his base. Notice how I have maintained a tight grip on his left sleeve.

I dig my left arm as deep as possible into Dave's left armpit, capturing him in the arm drag position. Once accomplished, I release my right grip on his sleeve and begin opening my guard.

I cup my left palm around Dave's left triceps. At the same time, I reach my right arm over his left arm and grab the seam on his right shoulder. Once accomplished, I use my right forearm to drive his head toward my right side.

I place my right foot on Dave's left hip and then use it as an anchor to turn my body in a clockwise direction. At the same time, I wrap my left leg over Dave's back and apply downward pressure. Still pushing on his head with my right forearm, his base collapses toward my right.

Continuing to drive Dave's head away from me using my right forearm, I begin to swing my right leg toward the right side of his head.

I swing my right leg to the right side of Dave's head. Applying downward pressure with both legs, I finish the arm bar by bridging my hips. It is important to notice that Dave's left arm is positioned off to my side instead of down the length of my chest. In order to hyperextend his arm from this position, my left elbow must be positioned above his right elbow. When accomplished, you will be able to apply even more pressure than with the standard arm bar.

ELBOW PRESSURE ARM BAR

A lot of times when you break your opponent down and establish a tight overhook on his arm, he will attempt to break your grip by posturing up. However, he will usually get stuck between the postured up and postured down positions for a brief moment, creating the perfect amount of space for you to attack with an arm bar. The key to being effective with this technique is speed and fluidity. Instead of placing your foot on your opponent's hip and angling your body off to the side, which can often give away your intentions, you establish your angle by underhooking his leg and pulling your body into position.

I have broken Dave down into my guard and established a whizzer control grip. My left arm is wrapped around his right arm above his elbow, and I've established a left grip on his left lapel to strengthen my hold. In an attempt to escape my control, Dave begins posturing up.

As Dave attempts to posture up, I hook my right arm around the inside of his left leg and then use it as an anchor to rotate my body in a counterclockwise direction.

Using my hook on Dave's left leg, I continue to rotate my body in counterclockwise direction and swing my left leg toward the left side of his head.

Having turned my body perpendicular to Dave's body, I swing my left leg to the left side of Dave's head. Notice how I've kept my left elbow clamped down above his right elbow.

Applying downward pressure with my legs, I slightly elevate Dave's left leg using my right arm to further disrupt his base. To finish the arm bar, I bridge my hips.

POSTURE LEG OVER ARM BAR

This technique is utilized in the same scenario as the last. You've broken your opponent down, established a tight overhook on his arm, and he is attempting to posture up to shatter your control. However, in this sequence your opponent is doing a better job at creating space using his free hand. Instead of attempting to close off that space, you use it to your advantage by throwing your legs over his head and crossing your feet, just as you would when closing your guard. Once accomplished, you can hyperextend his arm by simply bridging your hips. The key to success with this technique is maintaining a tight overhook. If you lose your opponent's elbow, clamp down on his wrist. It is also important to make sure your opponent is gaining posture before attempting this submission, as well as not bridging before you have crossed your legs. If you bridge prior to crossing your legs, you could be helping your opponent pass your guard.

I have broken Dave down into my guard and established a whizzer control grip. My left arm is wrapped around his right arm above his elbow, and I've established a left grip on his right lapel to strengthen my hold.

In an attempt to break my control, Dave posts his left hand on my chest and pushes his body upward. However, with his right arm trapped, he is unable to posture all the way up, creating the perfect opportunity for me to attack. To prevent him from dropping back down into my guard or further straightening his body, I reach my right arm up and grab his right collar.

Maintaining Dave's current posture using my right hand, I swing my left leg toward the front of his right shoulder.

As I position my left calf over Dave's right shoulder and my left foot in front of his face, I release my right grip on his collar. Using my left leg to push his head away from me, I swing my right leg toward the front of his body.

I hook my right leg over my left foot, trapping both of Dave's arms to the inside of his body.

Keeping my left arm wrapped tightly around Dave's right arm, I apply outward pressure with my legs and bridge my hips, hyperextending his elbow and forcing him to tap.

ARM BAR OFF AMERICANA

Sometimes your opponent will attempt a nontraditional technique while in your closed guard. This is especially true when he is a novice competitor or you've managed to thoroughly frustrate him. While his movements might be technically unsound, you must learn how to deal with them to avoid a defeat. In this scenario, your opponent attempts to isolate one of your arms and apply an Americana submission from your guard, which is frowned upon in jiu-jitsu. The first step when faced with this situation is to establish a cross grip on his far arm using your free hand. This anchor allows you to turn your body and head toward your trapped arm, alleviating the pressure from your shoulder. At the same time, open your guard and swing your leg over your opponent's head to assume the arm bar position. There is no need to place your foot on his hip. Since you've already turned your body using your cross grip, you can immediately swing your leg over and finish. The key to being successful with this technique is speed. I strongly suggest drilling this technique and others like it on a frequent basis. While it is important to train for people who have technically sound jiu-jitsu, it is just as important to train for people who throw the rules out the window. The last thing you want is to fall victim to a technically unsound submission or style.

As Dave postures up in my guard, he establishes a right grip on my collar and a left grip along my waistline. To keep my options open, I grip his wrists with my hands.

Dave grabs my right wrist with his left hand and then begins forcing my arm toward the mat.

Releasing his collar grip, Dave latches on to my right wrist with his right hand and pins my arm to the mat. Notice how he commits to the attack by dropping his right elbow to the mat on the right side of my head.

Dave slides his left hand underneath my right arm.

As Dave attempts to grab his right wrist with his left hand and lock in the Americana submission, I reach my left arm over his right arm and grab his left sleeve. In addition to helping me defend against the Americana, this grip allows me to begin turning my body in a counterclockwise direction.

I wrap my right leg around Dave's left side and then use it as an anchor to continue to turn my body in a counterclockwise direction. Once my body is perpendicular to his, I drive his head away from me using my left forearm and swing my left leg toward the left side of his head. It is important to note that this step must be executed quickly. If you delay, your opponent will most likely sense danger and release the Americana.

Realizing he is in danger, Dave abandons his submission. To capture him in an arm bar, I quickly wrap my right arm over his wrist and then wrap my left arm over my right arm. To finish the submission, I apply downward pressure with my legs and bridge my hips.

COUNTERING NECK CRANK TO ARM BAR

In this sequence your opponent attempts a can opener submission, which is where he plants his elbows on your chest, wraps his hands around the back of your head, and then forces your chin to your chest to put a tremendous amount of pressure on the back of your neck. It's an unorthodox submission, but you have to respect it or you could find yourself quickly tapping. The instant your opponent grabs your head, place your palms on his chin and straighten your arms. This will force your opponent away and prevent him from digging his elbows into your chest, thereby alleviating pressure from your neck. Having created space, place your foot on this hip, trap your opponent's straightened arms to your chest, angle off to the side, and then throw your leg over his head to finish the arm bar. The key to success is a quick reaction. The instant you drive your palms into your opponent's chin and straighten his arms, he will most likely realize his vulnerability. The goal is to transition into the arm bar before he releases control of your head.

As Dave postures up in my guard, he establishes a right grip on my collar.

Dave suddenly dives forward, clasps his hands around the back of my neck, posts his elbows on my chest, and applies a neck crank by pulling my chin toward my chest. The instant he does this, I angle my elbows out to my sides, cup my left palm underneath his chin, place my right palm over my left hand, and then force his head away from me and toward my left side.

Continuing to force Dave's head away from me, I lock my arms straight. Once my elbows are locked, it will be very difficult for him to reposition his elbows on my chest for leverage.

Opening my guard, I place my left foot on Dave's right hip and relax my right leg.

Driving off Dave's right hip using my left foot, I rotate my body in a counter-clockwise direction, slide my right leg up toward his armpit, and then apply downward pressure with my right leg. At the same time, I hook my right arm over his left elbow and apply downward pressure, trapping his left hand between my shoulder and head. Notice how my left arm is still locked to keep his head away from me.

Maintaining downward pressure with my right leg, I swing my left leg toward the left side of Dave's head.

As I hook my left leg around the left side of Dave's head, I pull my left palm away from his chin and then wrap my left arm over his left arm.

To finish the arm bar, I keep Dave's arms trapped to my chest, continue to apply downward pressure with my legs, and bridge my hips.

PENDULUM SWEEP

In this sequence your opponent defends against the arm bar by clasping his hands together, bending his trapped arm, and driving his weight forward to stack your legs over your body. This takes away much of your leverage, making it difficult to finish the submission. Instead of returning to closed guard, you use his forward pressure against him by forcing him into a shoulder roll and then claiming the mount position. The key to success with this technique is forcing your opponent in the proper direction. With both of his arms tied up with defense, he has three base points—both of his knees and his head. If you roll him toward any of those base points, he will be able to maintain his base and block the sweep. As a result, you want to force his body to roll between his knees and head, toward his shoulder.

As Dave postures up in my guard, he establishes a right grip on my collar and a left grip along my waistline. As I establish elbow control on his arms, he posts his left foot on the mat.

Maintaining my left grip on Dave's right sleeve, I hook my right hand underneath his left leg.

I open my guard, relax my right leg, use my hook to rotate my body in a counter-clockwise direction, and swing my left leg toward the left side of Dave's head.

As I wrap my left leg around the left side of Dave's head, I slide my left forearm over his right wrist to trap his arm to my chest.

Before I can bridge my hips and hyperextend Dave's arm, he drops his weight onto my legs and bends his trapped arm, making it difficult for me to finish the arm bar. Instead of fighting his superior leverage, I decide to use his defensive positioning to sweep him to his back.

I kick my left leg toward my left side and drive Dave in the same direction using my right leg. Notice how my head is now off-line from his forward pressure. Currently, he is driving toward the mat.

Turning toward my left side, I kick my left leg down to the mat, drive my right leg into Dave's left side, and begin pushing his left leg up and over his head using my right hand. It is important to notice that I still have his right arm trapped to my chest, preventing him from posting his hand on the mat and blocking the sweep.

Turning onto my left side, I force Dave to fall forward onto his shoulders using my right leg and right hand.

Continuing with my previous actions, I send Dave into a shoulder roll. As he comes down on his back, I turn my body to assume the mount position.

The instant I land in the mount, I secure the position by clamping my legs tight to Dave's hips, hooking my left arm around the back of his head, and posting my right hand out to my right side. It is important to note that if my head were on the opposite side of Dave's head, I would have wrapped my right arm around his head and posted my left hand on the mat.

ARM LOCK PENDULUM TO THE STANDARD ARM LOCK POSITION (S.A.P)

In this sequence you execute the same pendulum sweep as you did in the last sequence to deal with your opponent's arm bar defense, but instead of claiming the mount after sweeping him to his back, you finish the arm bar from the top position. To be successful with this technique, you must maintain control of your opponent's trapped arm as he rolls. It is also important to maintain your grip on his leg, as it will prevent him from scrambling and escaping the submission. Just as with the pendulum sweep, the technique is highly effective because instead of challenging your opponent's weight and leverage, you simply redirect it. The best part of this technique is that it lands you in the standard arm lock position, which means no scrambling to gain the top position.

As Dave postures up in my guard, he establishes a right grip on my collar and a left grip along my waistline. Immediately I grab his right sleeve above his elbow using my left hand.

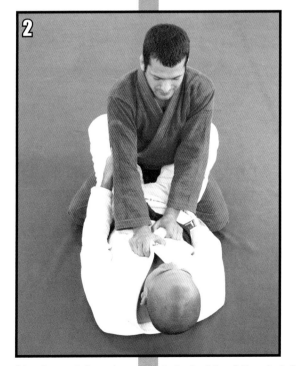

I hook my right palm around the inside of Dave's left leg.

Dave makes the mistake of posting his left foot on the mat instead of his right. As a result, I maintain my right hook around the inside of his left leg.

Using my right hook as an anchor, I rotate my body in a counterclockwise direction. Notice how I have maintained control of Dave's right elbow using my left hand.

Having assumed the angle I need to attack Dave's trapped arm, I hook my left leg around the left side of his head.

To defend against the arm bar, Dave drives his weight forward, bends his trapped arm, and then clasps his hands together.

Realizing that I won't be able to finish the arm bar, I transition into the sweep by kicking my left leg toward the mat, driving Dave in the same direction using my right leg, and punching his right leg up and over his head using my right hand.

I turn onto my left side, kick my left leg to the mat, and force Dave into a forward roll using my right leg and right hand.

As Dave rolls to his back, I do not follow him over to claim the mount position. Instead, I remain sitting off to his right side, hook my left forearm over his right wrist to trap his arm to my chest, and maintain my right grip on his left pants leg to prevent him from scrambling.

I wrap my left leg over Dave's face, lean back, and break his clasped hands apart by pulling his right arm into my chest using my left forearm.

Maintaining my right grip on Dave's left leg for control, I drop to my back, keep his right arm snug to my chest using the bend of my left arm, and apply downward pressure with my legs. To lock in the submission, I pinch my knees together and bridge my hips.

ARM BAR TO PENDULUM SWEEP TO ARM BAR

In the previous sequence I demonstrated how to sweep an opponent over to his back when he defends against the arm bar by clasping his hands together, driving his weight forward, and stacking your legs over your body. It's an effective move, but sometimes your opponent will defend against the sweep by positing his free hand on the mat. In such a situation, all you have to do is return to the arm bar. With your opponent's hands separated, his arm bar defense will be weakened, allowing you to throw your leg back over his head, isolate his trapped arm, and hyperextend his elbow.

As Dave postures up in my guard, he establishes a right grip on my collar and a left grip along my waistline. Immediately I grab his right sleeve above his elbow using my left hand.

Dave posts his left foot on the mat to stand up.

I grab the crook of Dave's left leg with my right hand and then use that anchor to rotate my body in a counterclockwise direction.

Once I've rotated my body perpendicular to Dave's body, I maintain a tight grip on his right elbow, open my guard, throw my left leg toward the left side of his head, and slide my right leg up to his left armpit.

Still rotating in a counterclockwise direction, I throw my left leg over Dave's head.

Still controlling Dave's right elbow with my left hand, I wrap my left leg around the left side of his head.

As I slide my left forearm down to Dave's right wrist to apply the arm bar, he senses the danger and drives his weight down into my legs, stacking me. This allows him to keep his right arm bent and avoid the arm bar.

I remove my left leg from Dave's head and throw it toward the mat to my left. In addition to this, I drive Dave in the same direction using my right leg.

As I continue with my previous actions, I punch Dave's left leg toward my left side using my right hand. Realizing he is about to get swept to his back, he counters by posting his left hand on the mat. Although this makes it difficult to finish the sweep, I have removed his weight from my body, allowing me to return to the arm bar. To make the transition, I straighten his right arm across my chest using my left arm and hook my left leg around the left side of his head.

To finish the arm bar, I pinch my knees together, apply downward pressure with my legs, and bridge my hips into Dave's right elbow. Notice how I keep his left leg off the mat using my right hand. This prevents him from once again driving his weight down on my legs and stacking me.

FOLLOW-THROUGH ARM BAR

This is another technique that can be employed when your opponent counters the arm bar by driving his weight into your legs and stacking you. Instead of remaining perpendicular to him and redirecting his downward pressure, you move away from his pressure. This is accomplished by rotating your body underneath him in an almost complete circle. By moving your body to the opposite side, your opponent's downward pressure will be directed toward the mat, making it easy to roll him over to his back and finish with the arm bar. In order to be effective with this technique, you must act quickly. The longer you stall in the arm bar position, the more downward pressure your opponent will apply. The goal is to sense the pressure coming and then rotate toward his far leg before he can stifle your movements. If you look at the photos below, you'll notice that I latch on to my opponent's far pant leg as I turn. This is a very important step because it not only allows you to lift his leg and complete your rotation, but it also prevents him from scrambling up to his knees after you force him to roll.

Dave postures up in my guard, establishing a right grip on my collar and a left grip along my waistline. As I grab his right sleeve above his elbow using my left hand, he posts his left foot on the mat.

I hook my right arm around the inside of Dave's left leg and then use the anchor to rotate my body in a counterclockwise direction.

I continue to rotate my body until I'm perpendicular with Dave. Maintaining control of his right arm using my elbow control, it is safe to open my guard and throw my left leg toward the left side of his head.

I wrap my left leg around the left side of Dave's head and pin his arm to my chest with my left arm, but before I can bridge my hips and hyperextend his elbow, he counters by driving his weight down into me, bending his trapped arm, and clasping his hands together.

Dave attempts to wrap his left arm around my head to hinder my movement and apply additional downward pressure. To block him from establishing this control, I place my right hand on top of my head. Notice how angling my arm outward serves as a deflector.

I grab Dave's right wrist with my right hand and then force his arm over my head and toward my left side.

7

Once I have cleared Dave's left arm over my head, I can freely hook my right arm around the outside of his right leg.

8

Using my hook on Dave's right leg, I rotate my body in a counterclockwise direction. Notice that by moving my body out from underneath him, his downward pressure has nothing to rest upon and causes him to begin falling forward.

9

I grab the bottom of Dave's right pant leg and then use that control to continue rotating my body in a counterclockwise direction.

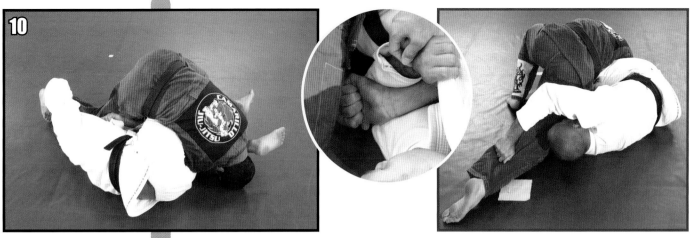

Dave's right leg is blocking me from popping my head out from underneath his body, so I use my grip on his pant leg to lift his leg upward. Once accomplished, I pull my head out so that my body is parallel with his. It is important to mention that I still have my left arm hooked over his right arm. To ensure he doesn't pull his arm out, I grab my right collar with my left hand.

I force Dave to roll over his right shoulder by driving into him with my legs and pulling his right leg over my body toward the mat.

As Dave rolls over his right shoulder and onto his back, I keep his right leg elevated to prevent him from posting his foot on the mat and rolling back on top of me.

As Dave lands on his back, I hyperextend his elbow by sliding my left arm up to his right wrist, applying downward pressure with my legs, pinching my knees together, and bridging my hips. To prevent him from scrambling, I maintain my right grip on his right pant leg.

BICEPS SLICER

In this scenario, you're up against an opponent with solid arm bar defense. He drives his weight into you to stack your legs, positions one foot up by your head to stop you from rotating underneath him, and maintains a solid base to hinder your sweeps. In addition to this, he locks his arms together with a rear naked choke grip to prevent you from straightening his arm and applying the arm bar submission. Instead of battling his leverage and weight for the arm bar, you use the defensive positioning of his arms to transition into the biceps slicer. This is accomplished by placing a leg into the gap between his arms, then applying downward pressure on his trapped arm with a triangle lock. As his trapped arm folds over your arm, it causes him an extreme amount of pain. Most of the time, this will produce one of three reactions. Your opponent will tap from the arm slicer, he'll straighten his arm to relieve pressure, allowing you to return to the arm bar, or he'll posture up, which allows you to roll him to his back and finish with the arm bar from the top position.

Dave postures up in my closed guard and posts his left foot on the mat. Immediately I grab his right sleeve above his elbow using my left hand and move my right arm toward the inside of his left leg.

I hook my right arm around the inside of Dave's left leg and begin rotating my body in a counterclockwise direction.

As I continue to rotate in a counterclockwise direction, I maintain control of Dave's right elbow, open my guard, throw my left leg toward the left side of his head, and slide my right leg up into his left armpit.

As I wrap my left leg around the left side of Dave's head, he realizes that I'm going for an arm bar and utilizes the rear naked choke defense. To accomplish this, he grabs his left biceps with his right hand and hooks his right hand over my left leg. In order to apply the arm bar, I need to straighten his right arm, but it is very difficult to do from this position.

To use Dave's defensive positioning to my advantage, I pull my right leg toward my head and then place my shin in the valley between his two elbows. At the same time, I drive his head downward using my left leg.

I hook the crook of my left leg over my right foot. Next, I bridge my hips and curl my left leg downward into my right foot. This forces my right calf down into Dave's right forearm, which in turn forces the bone of my left forearm down into his right biceps, causing him an extreme amount of pain.

COUNTERING STANDING DEFENSE

When you capture an opponent in an arm bar from your guard, sometimes he will grab the wrist of his trapped arm with his free hand, stand up, and attempt to shake you off of his arm. This is especially true with Judoka. In order not to fall victim to this defense, you want to keep your legs locked tightly around his head and body. This accomplishes two things—it makes it more difficult for him to increase his elevation, and if he should stand up, it ensures your body will remain attached to his arm, which means you'll get lifted off the mat. The straighter your opponent can stand, the more likely he'll be to escape the submission, so the instant your back comes off the mat, wrap your free arm around the inside of your opponent's near leg. This will keep his head bowed forward, put a lot of pressure on his back, and weaken the defensive grip he has with his free hand. Eventually one of two things will happen; you'll either manage to straighten your opponent's arm from the standing position or he will drop back down, in which case you can also finish the arm bar. The most important part of this technique is not getting rattled as you get lifted off the mat. As long as you keep everything nice and tight, the scenario will usually end up in your favor.

As Dave postures up in my guard, he establishes a right grip on my collar and a left grip along my waistline. Immediately I grab his sleeve above his right elbow using my left hand.

Dave posts his left foot on the mat. Immediately I hook my right hand around the inside of his left leg and then use that anchor to rotate my body in a counterclockwise direction.

Having rotated my body perpendicular to Dave's body, I maintain control of his right elbow, open my guard, throw my left leg toward the left side of his head, and slide my right leg up into his left armpit.

I hook my left leg around the left side of Dave's head.

Before I can bridge my hips and apply the arm bar, Dave defends by stacking his weight over my legs and bending his trapped arm.

Still stacking me, Dave clasps his hands together, climbs to both feet, and begins lifting me off the mat.

Keeping his hands clasped together and his right arm bent, Dave postures up. As he does this, I stay true to the technique by keeping my legs coiled tightly around his head and back and my right arm wrapped firmly around his left leg.

As Dave continues to posture up, I keep everything tight and begin bridging my hips into the back of his right arm. With my right arm wrapped around his left leg, it is impossible for him to stand up all the way, forcing him to remain bent over.

Unable to escape and burning excessive energy, his right arm eventually straightens, allowing me to finish the arm bar by bridging my hips.

DECOY SWEEP TO ARM BAR

When you fail to break your opponent's posture, there is a good chance that he will stand up to avoid your submissions and open your guard. It's certainly possible to apply an arm bar the instant he stands, but if you grab the arm you want to attack directly, there is a good chance he will defend against the submission. Sometimes a better approach is to use a decoy to mask your intentions. In this scenario, my goal is to attack my opponent's lead arm, but to lead him astray, I begin by establishing a cross grip on his rear sleeve and wrapping my opposite arm around his leg. This leads him to believe that I am attempting a sweep, causing him to post his lead hand on my chest as a brace. Still not attacking his lead arm, I pass his rear sleeve off to the hand I have wrapped around his leg, trapping his arm to his thigh. My opponent's most common reaction will be to drop down to his knees to avoid the sweep, but before he can accomplish this, I latch on to his lead arm with my free hand, throw my leg over his head, and apply the arm bar. With his rear hand tied up, he is unable to assume the rear naked choke defense, leading to an easy finish. The key to success with this technique is applying the arm bar before your opponent has a chance to drop back down to his knees.

As Dave postures up in my guard, he establishes a right grip on my collar and a left grip along my waistline. To prepare my defense, I establish a left grip on his right elbow and a right grip on his left sleeve.

Dave posts his right foot on the mat and begins to stand.

As Dave posts his left foot on the mat and stands up, I hook my left arm over his right arm and grab his left sleeve.

I wrap my right arm all the way around Dave's left leg and then pass his left sleeve from my left hand to my right hand. Notice how I have angled my head toward my right side.

I establish a firm grip on Dave's left sleeve using my right hand, trapping his arm to his leg.

I grab Dave's left collar using my left hand.

Preventing Dave from posturing up using my left grip on his collar, I open my guard and slide my right leg up his body toward his armpit. My actions make him think I am attempting to sweep him.

As Dave prepares to defend against the sweep, I quickly hook my left leg around the left side of his head and grab his right wrist with my left hand. To finish the arm bar, I apply downward pressure with my legs, keep his right arm trapped to my chest, and bridge my hips. With his left arm still pinned to his leg, he is unable to defend against the submission.

LADDER UP ARM BAR

This is a more traditional way to capture your opponent in an arm bar when he stands up in your closed guard. To pull it off effectively, you must maintain solid grips, walk your upper body between his legs, and climb your legs up his back. When you manage all three, your body will be almost vertical, putting you in a prime position to throw your leg over his head and apply the arm bar. The key to success is using your grips to prevent your opponent from posturing all the way up. The more he stands, the greater ability he has to open your guard and pass. Also, when opening your guard it is very important to pinch your knees together to keep your opponent trapped in the position. The nice part about traditional moves is that they are usually effective and easy to pull off. The downside is that they are taught most to jiu-jitsu practitioners, making them frequently countered.

As Dave stands up in my closed guard, I establish grips behind both of his elbows and pull his arms downward. Although his hips are still elevating, I want to pull his upper body into me as much as possible.

Continuing to pull Dave's upper body into me using my grips, I walk my shoulders toward his legs. Notice how this draws his weight forward.

Having repositioned my shoulders below Dave's hips, I open my guard and slide my left leg up his back toward his armpit. In addition to pulling his upper body toward me using my hands, I can now apply downward pressure using my leg.

Maintaining downward pressure with my left leg, I slide my right leg up Dave's back toward his armpit.

I release my right grip on Dave's left sleeve, hook my right arm around the inside of his left leg, and then use my hook to rotate my body in a counterclockwise direction. At the same time, I pinch my knees together, creating a vise that holds his upper body in place.

With my body now perpendicular to Dave's body, I swing my left leg toward the left side of his head.

I hook my left leg around the left side of Dave's head. To finish the submission, I slide my left arm over his right wrist, apply downward pressure with my legs, and bridge my hips to hyperextend his elbow.

FAKE SWEEP TO ARM BAR

This is another traditional technique that you can use to snare your opponent in an arm bar when he stands up in your closed guard. By grabbing his legs and driving into him, he will most likely establish firm grips on your lapel to prevent from falling backward. The instant he does this, latch on to one of his arms and transition into a straight arm bar. As I mentioned in the previous introduction, because traditional moves are trained in almost every academy, they are frequently countered. However, when you combine two or more traditional techniques together, your chances of success rise dramatically. The key to this technique is being explosive with the initial sweep to get your opponent to defend, and then making a smooth transition into the arm bar.

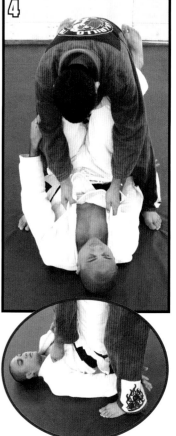

After establishing a right grip on my collar and a left grip along my waistline, Dave stands up in my closed guard. Instead of opening my guard, I keep my legs hooked together and allow my hips to be elevated off the mat. To set up the sweep, I wrap my hands around the back of his legs.

I slide my hands down to Dave's ankles, open my guard, and pinch my knees together. Next, I fake a sweep by pulling his ankles toward my head and driving into him using my legs. It is important to notice that although my knees are together, I still have my feet hooked around the outside of his waist.

To prevent from getting swept to his back, Dave uses his grips on my gi to pull his body forward. Immediately I reach my left hand up and grip his right sleeve above his elbow.

I let go of Dave's left ankle and hook my right arm around the inside of his left leg.

Using my hook on Dave's leg, I rotate my body in a counter-clockwise direction. At the same time, I kick my left leg toward the mat to help my rotation, pull his right elbow downward using my left hand, and wrap my right leg around his left side.

Having assumed the arm bar position, I swing my left leg toward the left side of Dave's head.

As I hook my left leg around the left side of Dave's head, I slide my left forearm down to his right wrist to trap his arm to my chest.

Using my right arm to maintain my angle, I finish the submission by applying downward pressure with my legs and bridging my hips. With Dave's arm trapped to my chest, his elbow gets hyperextended, forcing him to tap.

POSTURE BREAK ARM BAR

A lot of time when you break your opponent down, he will instinctively wrap an arm around your head in an attempt to gain control of your body. As long as you are quick to react, shrimping your body away from him will often straighten the arm he has wrapped around your head and trap his wrist between your head and shoulder. To hinder him from pulling his arm free, place your knee over his shoulder. With your opponent locked in place and your head acting as a fulcrum, hyperextending his elbow is as simple as applying downward pressure to his arm using your arms. The most important part of this technique is properly securing your opponent's shoulder with your knee and trapping his wrist between your head and shoulder. If you lose either point of control, he will most likely escape.

As Dave postures up in my guard, he establishes a right grip on my collar and a left grip along my waistline. To prepare my defense, I grab his sleeves above his elbows.

Using my grips, I pull Dave's elbows out to my sides and toward my head. The instant his elbows leave his core, his posture is weakened, allowing me to pull his upper body forward using my legs.

To prevent me from taking his back, Dave wraps his left arm around the back of my head, giving me a right underhook. To set up my offense, I wrap my right hand over his left shoulder.

I hook my right arm tightly over Dave's left shoulder to keep his arm trapped between my right shoulder and head, open my guard, shrimp my hips toward my right, and grab his right collar with my left hand.

As I continue to shrimp toward my right, I straighten my left arm. Because I have a left grip on Dave's right collar, this forces his head away from me, creating more space between us and straightening his left arm. At the same time, I begin sliding my right knee up his back toward his left shoulder.

 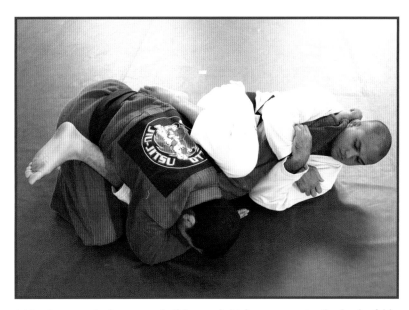

I slide my right knee over Dave's left shoulder to prevent him from posturing up and slide my right forearm up to the back of his left elbow. Next, I cross my left arm over my right arm. To apply the submission, I pull my arms downward into the back of his arm, hyperextending his elbow.

FAKE SIT-UP TO UNDERHOOK ARM BAR

When you're up against a technically sound opponent, it will be very difficult to catch him with a single attack. You must always launch a series of attacks. If he defends your first technique, you transition into a second. If he defends your second technique, you transition into a third. And you don't want to just string together random techniques. The attacks you choose should be based upon his counters. In this sequence I sit up into my opponent as though I'm attempting to execute a sweep, causing him to counter by driving his arms into me. The instant he does this, I establish an underhook on his near arm, trap his wrist between my shoulder and head, and apply the arm lock shown in the previous sequence. It's a very simple technique, but one many opponents overlook.

As Dave postures up in my guard, he establishes a right grip on my collar and a left grip along my waistline.

I post my left elbow on the mat, turn toward my left side, and grab Dave's right shoulder with my right hand. By turning onto my side instead of trying to sit straight up, his hands slide down my chest, weakening his posts.

Thinking that I am attempting to sweep him to his back, Dave drives his weight forward to counter. As he does this, I shoot my right hand underneath his left arm to establish an underhook.

As I slide my right arm underneath Dave's left arm, I turn my palm toward me. Notice how I'm still propped up on my left elbow.

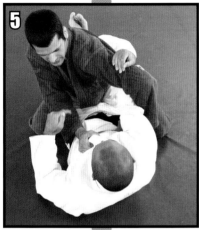

I cup my right hand over Dave's left triceps, curl my arm inward, and drop to my back. It is important to mention that this step must be done very quickly to prevent your opponent from pulling his arm away.

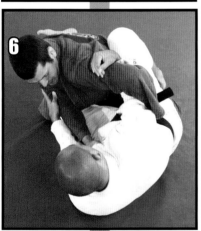

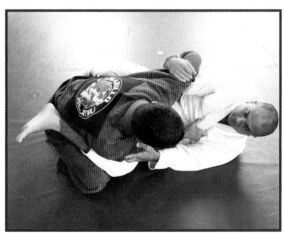

I open my guard, shrimp my hips toward my right, pull Dave's left arm toward me using my right hand, and begin sliding my right leg up his back toward his left shoulder. It is important to notice that my left leg is wrapped tightly around his right hip. This helps me shrimp my body away from him and create space.

Applying pressure to Dave's right hip using my left leg, I pull his left arm toward the right side of my head using my right arm. To secure my hold on his arm, I wrap my left hand over my right hand.

I slide my right knee over Dave's left shoulder to keep his posture broken, trap his left hand between the right side of my neck and right shoulder, and then crunch my body forward. To execute the submission, I apply downward pressure to his left elbow using my arms. This last step is important—if you do not put direct downward pressure on your opponent's elbow, you will most likely lose the submission.

FAKE SIT-UP TO UNDERHOOK ARM BAR 2

In this scenario you execute the same submission as in the previous two sequences, but your opponent manages to free his wrist from between your head and shoulder, eliminating your leverage on his elbow. Although it's great when you can finish your opponent with your first submission attempt, it is highly unlikely, especially when you're grappling with blue belts and above. In order to be successful, you must have a backup plan for every submission. In this case, you use your opponent's escape to roll directly into a straight arm bar. The key to success is not letting your opponent's arm make a connection with his head, which can be avoided by driving his face away with your hand as you make the transition. In this sequence, I have you finishing your opponent while he is on all fours. However, if he should roll to his back in an attempt to escape the submission, maintain control of his arm and roll with him. As long as you keep his arm pinned to his chest with his thumb pointing upward, you'll be in just as good of a position to hyperextend his elbow from your back.

I'm applying the arm bar demonstrated in the previous technique. My right knee is positioned over Dave's left shoulder to prevent him from posturing up, I've trapped his left wrist between my shoulder and head, and I'm applying downward pressure on his elbow using my arms.

Before Dave taps, he counters the submission by escaping his left wrist from between my shoulder and head. To deal with this scenario, I keep my right arm hooked tightly over his left arm and move my left arm toward his left wrist.

As I hook my left arm over Dave's left wrist, I shove his head away from me using my right hand to make it difficult for him to remove my dominant angle and force me to return to closed guard.

Turning over to assume a belly-down position, I drive my right shin into the back of Dave's head. It's possible for him to roll in this position, create a scramble, and escape the submission, so I act quickly.

To finish the submission, I keep Dave's left arm pinned to my chest and bridge my hips, hyperextending his arm. However, if he were to roll to his back in an attempt to escape the submission, I would roll with him in order to hold on to the arm bar.

WHIZZER GRIP TO KNEE PRESSURE ARM BAR

This is a very simple technique to employ when you establish a whizzer off a posture break. Instead of applying a submission that requires you to alter your grips, you maintain your whizzer grip and use it to lock in an arm bar. It's a quick submission that works great on strong opponent's who are masters at shattering your control while transitioning between grips.

As Dave postures up in my guard, he establishes a right grip on my collar and a left grip along my waistline. Immediately I grab a hold of his sleeves.

As I grab Dave's right sleeve with my right hand, I reach my left arm to the inside of his right arm. Notice how my elbows are tight to my body.

I slide my left elbow up to the crook of his right elbow and then force his arm upward, breaking his grip. At the same time, I use my right grip on his sleeve to pull his arm toward the back of my head.

Using my right grip on his sleeve, I pull Dave's hand behind my head. At the same time, I begin wrapping my left arm around his right arm above his elbow. To further disrupt his posture, I pull him forward using my legs.

With Dave broken down, I wrap my left arm tightly around his right arm, establishing a whizzer. Immediately I grab his right lapel with my right hand and begin passing it toward my left hand.

After passing off Dave's right lapel from my right hand to my left, I place my right hand on his left biceps and force him away from me. At the same time, I open my guard and place my left foot on the mat.

Using my left foot and right hand as anchors, I shrimp my body to my left to create space. Notice how I have maintained a tight whizzer on his right arm above his elbow.

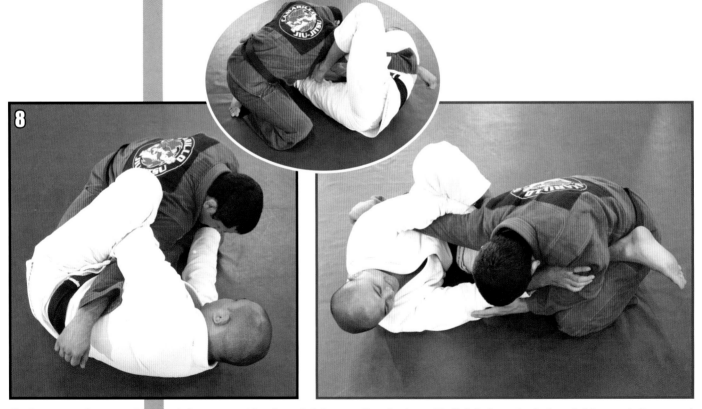

Having created space with the shrimp move, I hook my left foot on Dave's chest. To finish the submission, I drive my left arm and left knee down into his trapped arm, hyperextending his elbow. Notice how I have kept my right arm locked straight to prevent him from driving into me and escaping the submission.

WINDMILL BREAK TO KIMURA

This techniques begins by shattering your opponent's posts, but instead of accomplishing this by establishing grips on his sleeves, you slide your arms between your opponent's arms, and then fling your arms toward the outside of your body. If you manage to strip his grips, his body will fall forward and he'll place his hands on the mat. This presents a perfect opportunity to grab one of his wrists and sit up into him to execute a sweep. Sometimes you will be successful and put your opponent on his back, and other times he will counter the sweep by driving his weight back into you. If the latter occurs, you'll have a perfect opportunity to isolate one of his arms and lock in the kimura. The key to success is transitioning into the kimura the instant your opponent defends your sweep. If you're slow to react, he will realize your intentions and counter the submission. It is also important to angle your body out to the side once you've established your kimura grip. With your body perpendicular to his, you can apply the maximum amount of pressure to his shoulder, increasing your chances of finishing him with the submission.

As Dave postures up in my guard, he establishes a right grip on my collar and a left grip along my waistline. To begin my attack, I shoot my hands underneath his arms.

In one explosive movement, I dive my arms underneath Dave's arms, bring my hands together, and then force my arms away from my body to open his elbows and break his grips. Notice how as his posts weaken his body begins to fall forward.

As I force Dave's elbows toward the outside of my body, I pull him forward using my legs, causing him to place his left hand on the mat.

With both of his grips broken, Dave's weight carries his body forward and he places his right hand on the mat. Immediately I grab his left wrist with my right hand. Notice how I have kept my left arm to the inside of his right arm.

Posting on my right elbow, I lift my left shoulder off the mat and turn toward my right. Notice how my left elbow is tight to my body. From here, it looks like I'm setting up to sweep Dave toward my right, so he defends by driving his weight into me.

I wrap my left arm over Dave's left triceps, dig my forearm underneath his arm, and then grab my right wrist with my left hand.

As Dave drives his weight into me, I open my guard and place my right foot on his left hip. Using my right foot as an anchor, I rotate my body in a counterclockwise direction as I drop to my back. To prevent him from posturing up and escaping the submission, I apply downward pressure on his left elbow using my left arm.

Having shrimped my body perpendicular to Dave's body so that he can no longer put his weight on me, I slide my right knee up his back and over his left shoulder. As I apply downward pressure with my knee, his head collapses to the mat. If you fail to put a considerable amount of downward pressure on your opponent, he will most likely posture up or roll to escape the submission. To apply the kimura, I keep my elbows locked tight to my sides and use my right hand to drive Dave's wrist toward the back of his head.

SIT-UP SWEEP TO KIMURA

When an opponent postures up in your closed guard, the longer he can keep you pinned flat on your back, the easier it will be for him to open your guard. However, it is difficult for him to maintain solid grips at all times, especially late in the fight. To find his moments of weakness, I'll often mix my grips up and play possum. The instant I feel him relax, I'll make my charge by establishing a cross grip on his far shoulder, posting an elbow on the mat, and turning onto my side. With one shoulder angled up and the opposite one angled down, my opponent's hands slide down the slope of my chest, making it difficult for him to keep me pinned. Utilizing my suddenly mobility, I execute a sit-up sweep. To counter, he posts his hand on the mat, allowing me to isolate one arm and apply a kimura lock. Although this seems like a simple technique, it can be very difficult to pull off when your opponent has his hands posted on your chest. Having the ability to feel your opponent's weaknesses is mandatory.

As Dave postures up in my guard, he establishes a right grip on my collar and a left grip along my waistline. Immediately I grab his sleeves.

I post my right elbow on the mat, turn toward my right side, and grab Dave's left shoulder with my left hand. By turning onto my side instead of trying to sit straight up, I force his hands to slide toward my right side, and his grips weaken.

Continuing to sit up, I post my right hand on the mat behind me. Thinking I am attempting to sweep him to my right, Dave counters by posting his left hand on the mat. Although he prevented me from executing the sweep, he has made himself vulnerable to a shoulder lock.

Opening my guard, I post my feet on the mat and elevate my hips into Dave's body. With my weight driving into him, Dave commits more to his sweep counter by posting more heavily on his left hand.

Using my left foot and my left grip on Dave's left shoulder, I pull myself into his body. Now that I have access to his left arm, I drop down to my right elbow and grab his left wrist with my right hand. It is important to note that I have kept my right leg tight to his body to prevent him from further opening my guard.

I hook my left arm over Dave's left triceps, dive my left forearm underneath his left arm, and then grab my right wrist with my left hand, establishing a kimura grip. It is important to mention that my entire body is focused on isolating and controlling his left arm.

As I drop back toward my right side, I shift from my right hip toward my left hip. To set up the submission, I pull Dave's left shoulder downward using my left arm and force his left wrist along an upward arc toward the back of his head using my right hand.

Twisting my upper body toward my left side, I slide my right knee toward Dave's left shoulder and apply downward pressure to force his head toward the mat and prevent him from posturing up. To finish the submission, I apply downward pressure to his left elbow using my left arm and drive his left hand toward the back of his head using my right hand. It is important to note that when executing the kimura, the farther you can separate his trapped arm away from his body, the weaker his defense will be.

CLOSED-GUARD SHOULDER LOCK

This is another quick and easy submission that you can apply when you establish a whizzer grip off a posture break. With your opponent's wrist already trapped in your armpit, all the submission requires is to shrimp your body to the side and drive his elbow inward using your arm. This forces his arm to bend painfully against the joint, forcing him to tap. Utilizing quick submissions such as this one allows you to conserve energy and avoid the long, drawn-out process of finishing your opponent. It's also a good technique to have in your arsenal if you plan on competing in no-gi grappling or MMA because it doesn't involve gripping your opponent's gi.

I have broken Dave down and established a whizzer on his right arm. To lock my overhook tight, I grab his right collar with my left hand and tuck my left elbow to my body.

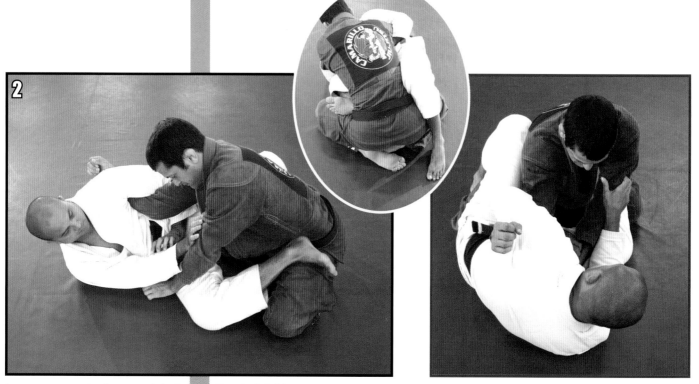

I open my guard, place my right foot on Dave's left hip, post my left foot on the mat, turn onto my right side, and then shrimp my hips toward my left. These actions cause his right elbow to slip off my left hip toward the inside of my body. To move his elbow even farther down my chest, I release my left grip on his collar and drive my left hand toward my right wrist.

With my right hand still cupped around Dave's left biceps, I grab my right wrist with my left hand. This prevents him from moving his right elbow toward the outside of my body. It is important to notice that his right wrist is trapped in my left armpit.

Turning toward my back, I force Dave's left elbow toward the center of my body using my left arm. As his arm bends, it puts a tremendous amount of pressure on his shoulder, causing him to tap. It is very important to notice that I still have my right foot on his left hip. As long as you control your opponent's hips, he won't be able to drive into you or circle, making it very difficult for him to defend against the shoulder lock.

SHOULDER LOCK OFF ARM BAR

In this sequence you latch on to your opponent's rear arm to execute an arm bar, but before you can assume the arm bar position, he counters by pulling his elbow away from you. This is the most traditional defense to the arm bar, and if you've already attacked his elbow several times in a fight, he'll most likely utilize it the instant you secure control of his arm. Although pulling his elbow out of the equation makes it difficult to finish the standard arm bar, it creates a pathway for you to climb your leg over his shoulder and establish a shoulder lock. As long as you still have control of his trapped arm, you'll be able to bridge and bend his arm backward over your thigh, putting a tremendous amount of pressure on his shoulder. The key to being successful with this technique is not dramatically opening your guard. Instead of throwing your legs wide, keep them tight to your opponent's body and then quickly hook your feet back together once you've snared his shoulder.

As Dave postures up in my guard, he establishes a right grip on my collar and a left grip along my waistline. Immediately I grab his left wrist with my right hand. At the same time, I begin sliding my left arm underneath his right arm.

I hook my left hand around Dave's left elbow, establishing the standard elbow lock position.

Pulling on Dave's left elbow using my left hand, I open my guard, swing my legs upward, hook the crook of my right leg over his left shoulder, and then close my guard tight. Next, I pinch my right knee close to his left ear and apply downward pressure with my legs.

I grab Dave's left wrist with my right hand to trap his arm to my chest and then bridge my hips to apply a straight arm lock. To counter, he pulls his trapped arm toward him and manages to escape his elbow. If I were to hang on to the straight arm bar, I would only burn energy, so I decide to use his positioning to capture him in a shoulder lock.

Using my hands, I pull Dave's left wrist over my right thigh toward my left side, causing his arm to bend unnaturally. With a ton of pressure being put on to his left shoulder, he taps in submission.

COLLAR POSTURE BREAK TO OMOPLATA

In this sequence I demonstrate how to break your opponent's posture and transition into the omoplata submission. Even if you're one of the many jiu-jitsu practitioners who have trouble finishing your opponent with the omoplata, it's not in your best interest to ignore this technique and the other setups I offer. As you will see in the coming section, obtaining the omoplata position creates an opening for a number of different submissions. Your primary goal should be to finish the omoplata, which I demonstrate how to accomplish at the end of this sequence, but if the omoplata should fail, you can use your opponent's counter to attack his foot, elbow, or wrist. However, none of these options become available unless you first master the omoplata position setups.

As Dave postures up in my guard, he establishes a right grip on my collar and a left grip along my waistline. Immediately I grab his sleeves.

Turning toward my right side, I reach my left hand over Dave's right arm and grab his left collar. By turning onto my side, his hands slide down my chest, weakening his posts.

Using my right grip, I roll Dave's left elbow away from his body, weakening his rear post. At the same time, I use my left collar grip to pull him toward my left side, open my guard, and pull my right knee forward to add pressure to his left shoulder.

Making my left leg heavy against Dave's right hip, I shrimp my hips to my right. It is important to mention that my right knee is still applying forward pressure to his left shoulder, I'm still pulling on his left arm using my right hand, and I'm still pulling on his collar using my left hand.

I hook my right leg over Dave's left shoulder. Notice how I have maintained my grip on his collar.

I release my left collar grip, drive Dave's head away from his arm using my right foot, and begin rotating my body in a counterclockwise direction.

Still driving Dave's head away from his arm using my right foot, I rotate in a counterclockwise direction and I pull my left leg out from underneath his body. It is important to notice that my right foot is flat on the mat. If you leave space between your foot and the mat, you give your opponent an opportunity to lift your leg over his head and escape the submission.

Still applying downward pressure to Dave's left shoulder to prevent him from posturing up, I straighten my right leg, post my left elbow on the mat, and begin sitting up.

I post my left hand on the mat, sit all the way up, and hook my right arm over Dave's back to prevent him escaping the submission by executing a forward roll. It is important to mention that I'm putting a lot of downward pressure on his left shoulder to break him down to the mat. If your opponent resists, kicking your leg toward the mat will usually do the trick.

I coil my right leg toward my body and then hook my right foot underneath my left leg. Notice how my body is perfectly parallel to Dave's body.

I grab the back of Dave's collar with my left hand, coil my left leg over my right foot, and pull my body toward his right shoulder. To apply the submission, I continue to pull my upper body toward his right shoulder and pull my feet toward his legs. These actions bend his arm backward, putting a tremendous amount of pressure on his shoulder.

STANDING IN POSTURE TO OMOPLATA ★ BJ FAVORITE

With my opponent postured up in my closed guard, I begin this sequence by executing a standard sit-up sweep. However, as my hips come off the mat, I begin pulling my right leg behind me, making my opponent believe that I'm attempting to escape back to my feet. To prevent me from achieving this goal, he wraps his left arm around right leg and attempts to pin it back to the mat. Although his actions make it difficult for me to stand, it allows me to rotate my body off to his side and lock up his left arm in the omoplata position. In order to be successful with this technique, the instant your opponent grabs your leg, drop your hips on the same side of his body that you're attacking. For example, in the sequence below my opponent wraps his left arm around my right leg, so I drop my hips to his left side. This allows me to angle my body off to the side, wrap my leg over his left shoulder, and finish the submission. If I were to drop my hips toward his right side, I would need to readjust them before applying the omoplata, costing me the element of surprise.

As Dave postures up in my guard, he establishes a right grip on my collar and a left grip along my waistline. Immediately I establish elbow control.

I post my right elbow on the mat, prop my body upright, turn toward my right side, and establish a left grip on Dave's left collar. Notice how I have slid my fingers into his collar but left my thumb on the outside.

I post my right hand on the mat, pull Dave toward me using my left collar grip to disrupt his posture, and continue to sit up.

Having pulled Dave toward me using my left collar grip in the previous step, he instinctively pulls away. The instant he does this, I post on my right hand and left foot, open my guard, relax my right leg, and elevate my hips off the mat.

Realizing that I am making an escape to my feet, Dave drives his weight forward and hooks his left arm around my right leg to prevent me from accomplishing my goal. As he does this, I use my left collar grip to pull his body toward my left side.

Dropping down to my back so that my body is perpendicular to Dave's body, I continue to pull him toward my left side using my cross collar grip and then hook my right leg over his left shoulder. It is important to note that because my opponent was grabbing my right leg, the transition came very easy.

I hook my left leg over my right foot and wrap my right arm around the back of Dave's left leg, securing the omoplata position.

I sit up, hook my right arm over Dave's back, and pull my body toward his right shoulder. From here, I can finish the omoplata.

WHIZZER GRIP TO FAKE CHOKE TO OMOPLATA

In this sequence, I break my opponent down and establish a tight whizzer on his right arm. However, instead of securing the whizzer by grabbing his near collar, as I did in several of the techniques earlier in the book, I reach my overhook hand across his torso and grab his far collar, establishing a choke position. To apply pressure to the choke, I drive his head away from me using my free arm. The more I push his head away, the deeper his collar digs into his throat. It's possible to finish your opponent with this rudimentary submission, but a lot of times he will push on the arm you're using to drive his head away to relieve pressure from his neck. Rather than burn unnecessary energy holding on to the choke, transition to the omoplata. This is accomplished by shrimping your body away from him, turning onto your side, and throwing your leg over the shoulder of his trapped arm. Getting your leg over your opponent's shoulder is usually the trickiest part, but with his head already shoved away from his arm due to the choke, this is usually fairly easy to manage. The key to success with this technique is maintaining a tight whizzer so you don't lose control of your opponent's elbow. It is also important to maintain the chokehold until you secure the omoplata position because it will disguise your transition.

As Dave postures up in my guard, he establishes a right grip on my collar and a left grip along my waistline. Immediately I grab his sleeves.

I establish a right grip on Dave's right sleeve, doubling up on his arm.

To break Dave's lead grip, I pull his right arm behind my head using my right hand, turn toward my right side, pull him forward using my legs, and shoot my left arm straight up to the inside of his right arm. Notice how the back of my left arm is lined up with the crook of his right arm, as well as how my left elbow is above his right elbow.

Keeping Dave's left hand behind my head using my right grip, I wrap my left arm over his arm and dig my left hand underneath his armpit. It is important to notice that I have wrapped up his arm above his elbow.

Once I have established a tight whizzer, I grab Dave's right collar with my right hand and then feed it to my left hand.

With my left palm facing toward me, I slide my fingers underneath Dave's collar and establish a tight grip. The higher up you can grab on your opponent's collar, the better.

I establish a grip on Dave's right shoulder with my right hand and then drive the blade of my forearm into the right side of his neck to force his chin and head toward my right side. As my right forearm drives into his right carotid artery, his left collar drives into his left carotid artery, severing blood flow to the brain. Notice how my elbows are tight to my body. If you utilize proper form and are able to apply a substantial amount of pressure, it is possible to finish the choke from this position.

Using his left hand, Dave drives my right elbow toward my left side to relieve pressure from his neck.

Dave is successful at relieving pressure from the choke. Before he switches from survival mode into an escape, I must transition into the omoplata. Continuing to apply pressure to the choke, I open my guard, place my left foot on his right hip, and relax my right leg.

Using my left foot on Dave's hip as an anchor, I shrimp my hips toward my left side. To create even more space, I continue to drive his head away from me using my right arm. It is important to notice that I still have a tight whizzer above his right elbow.

I slide my left knee over Dave's right shoulder.

Still isolating Dave's right arm by driving his head away from me using my right hand, I hook my left leg over the back of his right shoulder. To prevent him from posturing up, I apply downward pressure.

Now using my left foot to force Dave's head away from me, I release the choke, post my right elbow on the mat, and prop myself up. To prevent him from escaping by jumping his legs over my body in a counterclockwise direction, I extend my left arm over his back.

As I drive my left foot into the side of Dave's head, I create the space I need to pull my right leg out from underneath his body.

Extending my right leg out in front of me, I use my right hand to sit up and then wrap my left arm over Dave's back to prevent him from rolling. From here, I can finish the omoplata.

STANDING TO OMOPLATA ★ BJ FAVORITE

This technique is similar to the decoy sweep to arm bar shown earlier in the book in that the instant your opponent stands up in your guard, you put one of his arms out of commission by pinning it to his leg. If you look at the first photo in the sequence, you'll notice that I accomplish this by wrapping my right arm around the inside of his left leg and then grabbing his left sleeve with my right hand. Unable to use his trapped arm for defense, you have a couple of options. You can use the decoy sweep to arm bar to attack his elbow or you can employ this technique to transition to the omoplata and attack his shoulder.

As Dave stands up in my closed guard, I establish a left cross grip on his left collar, wrap my right arm around the inside of his right leg, and grab his left sleeve with my right hand. To see how this is accomplished, visit the "decoy sweep to arm bar" technique shown earlier in the book. To hinder him from elevating his head above his hips, I pull his collar toward me using my left hand and keep my legs locked together.

To separate Dave's head from his left arm, I use my cross collar grip to push his head toward my left side. Notice how I lead this movement with my left elbow.

Opening my guard, I place my left foot on Dave's right hip and throw my right leg over his left shoulder. To prevent him from pulling his right arm free, I maintain a very tight grip on his sleeve using my right hand.

I hook the crook of my left leg over my right foot, release my collar grip, and pull Dave's left leg between my right shoulder and head to make it difficult for him to remain standing. To drive his head toward the mat, I kick my left leg down into my right leg, causing my right leg to drive downward into his left shoulder.

As I drive my left foot to the mat, the pressure on Dave's left shoulder collapses him to the mat. To prevent him from rolling and escaping the omoplata position, I keep my right arm hooked around his left leg and maintain a tight right grip on his left sleeve.

Once I have Dave under control, I quickly pull my right arm out and wrap it over his back to prevent him from rolling. To finish the submission, I sit up and pull my upper body toward his right shoulder, putting extreme pressure on his left shoulder.

TOE HOLD FINISH

A lot of times when you secure the omoplata position, you'll be lying flat on your back with control of your opponent's near leg. In order to lock in the omoplata submission and apply pressure to his shoulder, you must release control of his leg, sit up, and throw an arm over his back to prevent him from rolling. Sometimes these steps are easy to manage, but not always. They can be quite a chore when your opponent is feisty or a good deal stronger than you. If your opponent won't let you sit up, and you know he will instantly pop up should you attempt to transition from the omoplata position to his back, a good option is to maintain your triangle lock on his arm and attack his near foot using the technique demonstrated below. It doesn't look like much, but it can put your opponent in agony in a split second.

Utilizing the previous technique, I've trapped Dave's left arm and have broken him down to the mat. Instead of sitting up to apply the omoplata submission, I decide to employ a foot lock from my current position.

Maintaining downward pressure on Dave's left shoulder using my right leg, I release my right grip on his left sleeve and grab the outside of his left foot so that my fingers are wrapped over his toes. At the same time, I grab his left heel with my left hand.

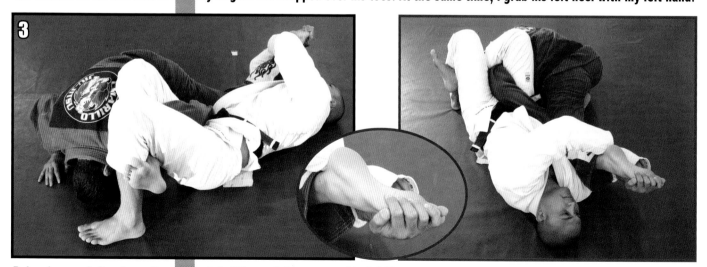

Releasing my left grip on Dave's heel, I slide my left arm over his Achilles tendon and grab my right wrist using my left hand. It is important to note that my left palm is facing upward. Once I've establish the kimura grip on his foot, I keep his leg stationary while I use my grip to push the toes of his left foot toward his left heel.

OMOPLATA TO WRIST LOCK

The omoplata submission is often difficult to finish, especially when up against a flexible or strong opponent, but it's still a highly advantageous position due to the number of different finishes that can be employed. In the previous sequence I demonstrated how to attack your opponent's near foot, and in this sequence I demonstrate how to attack his trapped wrist. In order to be successful with this technique, it is important to employ both hands. If you look at the photos below, you'll notice that I grab my opponent's wrist with my left hand to stabilize his arm and then bend his fingers downward using my right hand.

I was able to sit up in the omoplata position, but I'm having trouble finishing the shoulder lock. Because I'm already sitting up and Dave is completely sprawled out, making it difficult for him to roll, I decide to transition into a wrist lock.

I establish a left grip on Dave's right sleeve to keep his arm trapped and then lean slightly back. Notice how I still have my right arm hooked over his body to prevent him from rolling.

I cup my right palm on the top of Dave's hand and then drive his fingers toward his forearm. At the same time, I use my left sleeve grip to push his left wrist toward my right palm, putting even more pressure on the lock.

STRAIGHT ARM WRIST LOCK OFF OMOPLATA ★ BJ FAVORITE

In this scenario, your opponent is not only resisting the omoplata submission, but also using small movements to gradually escape the position. Instead of continuing with the omoplata, you drop to your back so that your body is perpendicular to his body and attack his trapped wrist. The best part about this submission is how it isolates your opponent's elbow and wrist away from his body. When you reposition your body, your opponent's arm straightens, making his wrist easily accessible. The key to being successful with this technique is hooking your foot in your opponent's far armpit. This gives you a connection to both sides of his body, making it very difficult for him to roll and escape the submission.

I have established the omoplata position and I'm leaning forward to finish the submission. However, Dave has both of his knees on the mat, giving him the leverage he needs to resist.

Dave posts his right hand on the mat and then pushes off to elevate his head. Although I have his shoulder locked up, as long as he is on his knees, he has more leverage off the mat than I do. Instead of battling him for the submission, I decide to transition into plan B and employ the straight arm wrist lock. Still applying downward pressure to his shoulder using my legs, I lean back and post my left hand on the mat.

As Dave continues to elevate his head off the mat, I drop to my back, hook my left foot underneath his right armpit, and hook my right foot underneath his head. It is important to notice that I am no longer parallel with his body. I've dropped back so that my body is perpendicular to his.

As I straighten my legs, additional pressure is applied to Dave's left shoulder, collapsing his upper body to the mat.

To apply even more pressure to Dave's left shoulder, I post my left hand on the mat behind me and sit up. Notice how his left arm is still hooked over my right thigh.

With Dave's right hand more exposed than it was when my body was parallel with his, I cup my right palm over the top of his hand. To apply the wrist lock, I force his fingers toward his body.

STRAIGHT ARM BAR FROM LEG HOOK

In this scenario, my opponent is doing an excellent job defending against the omoplata from the turtle position. To escape the submission all together, he posts his far foot on the mat and begins increasing the elevation of his hips. To block his escape, I drop perpendicular to his body as I did in the previous move, but instead of hooking my foot in his far armpit, I hook it underneath his posted leg. This allows me to once again secure an excellent trap on his arm and shoulder. The more he attempts to posture up, the more pressure gets applied to his shoulder. With his elevation gain halted, I finish the shoulder lock by scooting my body away from his and crunching my body forward.

I have established the omoplata position and I'm leaning forward to finish the submission. However, Dave has both of his knees on the mat, giving him the leverage he needs to resist.

Using his leverage off the mat to his advantage, Dave starts elevating his head. Immediately I reinforce my position by turning my body perpendicular to his and posting my hands on the mat behind me.

Dave posts his right hand on the mat and elevates his head. Once he's created space, he posts his right foot on the mat in front of him in an attempt to stand. Although being perpendicular to his body will make it difficult for me to finish the omoplata, I now have access to the far side of his body and begin moving my right foot toward the inside of his right leg.

Dropping to my back, I hook my right foot around the crook of Dave's right leg. This locks his left shoulder tight; if he attempts to move or stand from this position, additional pressure will be applied to his left shoulder.

To increase pressure on Dave's left shoulder, I straighten my left leg, scoot my butt away from him, and crunch my body forward by coming up onto my hands. Before I can crunch my body all the way forward, he taps.

OMOPLATA TO TRIANGLE

When you establish the omoplata position, the most common escape is for your opponent to lift his head. Using your legs to apply downward pressure to his shoulder is an excellent way to hinder this defense, but occasionally your opponent will overpower your control. As he elevates his body, your legs also get lifted off the mat, stealing the leverage you need to finish the submission. In such a scenario, an excellent way to combat this heavily utilized defense is to transition into a triangle as your opponent postures. The most important aspect of this technique is timing. If you look at the fourth photo in the sequence below, you'll notice that I wait for my opponent to elevate his head to a forty-five-degree angle before I wrap my leg around the back of his neck and begin setting up the triangle. If you make your move too soon or too late, your chances of making a successful transition drop dramatically. It is also important to quickly lock your feet together once you've shot the triangle. The longer you keep your legs open, the more opportunity your opponent will have to pass your guard.

Having assumed the omoplata position, I post my left hand on the mat and attempt to sit up and lean my weight toward Dave's right shoulder to finish the submission.

With leverage on his side, Dave posts his right hand on the mat and lifts his head upward, forcing me to my back. To prevent from losing the position, I quickly grab his belt with my right hand and latch on to his upper left sleeve using my left hand.

Dave continues to elevate his head. If I don't do something quick, he will be able to stand up and pull his trapped arm free.

Before Dave can stand, I begin hooking my left leg around the right side of his head. It is very important that I make this transition while he is still posting on his right arm. If he were to remove his weight from his hand before I made this transition, he would have access to my left leg. It is also important to note that I am still holding his belt with my right hand and applying downward pressure to his left shoulder using my right leg.

I wrap my left leg around the right side of Dave's head and then hook my feet together to assume the closed-guard triangle position. At the same time I release my grip on his belt and grab his left sleeve with my right hand. It is important to note that crossing your feet is vital—if you unhook your feet, your opponent could pull his arm free and escape the submission.

I bridge my hips upward to create the space I need to force Dave's left arm across my body using my grips.

Having crossed Dave's left arm to the left side of my body, I apply downward pressure to the back of his neck using my left leg.

For the triangle to be effective, I need to position my left leg over the back of Dave's neck. I accomplish this task by releasing my right grip on his sleeve, grabbing my left shin with my right hand, and then pulling my leg down so that it is positioned horizontally over the back of his neck.

I hook the crook of my right leg over my left foot.

To finish the submission, I squeeze my knees together, curl my right leg downward, and pull Dave's head into me using my right hand.

OMOPLATA TO STRAIGHT ARM BAR

When you establish the omoplata position, you drape one arm over your opponent's back to control his body and prevent him from escaping the position by executing a forward roll. The tighter the trap you have on his body, the better, but when up against a particularly strong grappler, occasionally he will be able to overpower your trap and roll over his shoulder to his back. With his arm still trapped between your legs, it's possible to counter this defense by transitioning into an arm bar. To accomplish this, lock your feet together to isolate his arm, grab his wrist, and then straighten his arm down the length of your chest. As he completes his roll and comes down onto his back, you'll be in a prime position to immediately slap on the arm bar. It is a very simple transition, but speed is of the utmost importance. If you wait until he reaches his back to make the transition, he will most likely pull his arm free. To be effective, you must begin setting up the arm bar the instant he begins to roll. The most important aspect of this technique is the tightness of your legs. If they are loose, your opponent will roll away, get up to his knees, and maintain the top position.

I've established the omoplata position. My right hand is over Dave's back to prevent him from rolling, and my left hand is posted behind me to keep my weight forward.

Determined to escape the omoplata, Dave executes a hard forward roll. Although my goal is to allow him to roll so I can catch him in an arm bar, I don't want him to head into his roll with a lot of momentum. Accordingly, I use my right arm to slow his body, but pull it out of the picture before he abandons his escape.

Having pulled my right arm back, Dave sees a pathway to escape and continues with his forward roll. To set him up for the arm bar, I keep my legs locked tight around his left arm. If I feel that things are going badly from this position, I can still obtain the top position by getting to my knees or standing.

Having slowed down Dave's forward roll, I manage to maintain control of his left arm as he rolls to his back. To begin applying the submission, I grab his left sleeve above his elbow using my left hand, latch on to his wrist with my right hand, and straighten his arm as I drop to my back.

With my feet hooked tightly together underneath Dave's back, I straighten his arm across my chest using my hands and then hyperextend his elbow by bridging my hips. It is important to notice that I have turned his left wrist so that his thumb is pointing upward.

OMOPLATA ROLL TO STRAIGHT KNEE LOCK

Just like the previous technique, this move can be utilized from the omoplata position in a couple of scenarios: when your opponent overpowers the trap you have on his body by executing a forward roll or you're having no luck finishing him with the shoulder lock and remove your arm from his back to bait him into a forward roll. Deciding whether to utilize this technique or the straight arm bar boils down to the direction in which your opponent rolls. Instead of rolling straight over to his back, as your opponent did in the previous sequence, he turns into you as he rolls in an attempt to put you into his guard. Although this doesn't give you great access to his arm, making it difficult to apply the straight arm bar, it gives you access to his near leg, allowing you execute a knee lock. If you look at the second photo in the sequence below, you'll notice that I grab the waistline of my opponent's pants as he goes over. This not only allows me to steer his roll, but it also allows me to slow the momentum behind his roll, which makes the submission easier to apply.

I've established the omoplata position. My right hand is over Dave's back to prevent him from rolling, and I'm gripping his left sleeve above his elbow with my left hand to prevent him from pulling his arm free.

To set up the straight knee lock, I pull my right arm off of Dave's back and allow him to execute a forward roll. However, at the same time, I grab his uniform along his lower back with my left hand and slow his roll by holding his body up.

By controlling the speed of Dave's forward roll using my left hand, I create the opportunity to wrap my right arm around his lower left leg and pull it into my body. To further isolate his left leg from his body, I drive my right leg into his left hip.

I grab Dave's left ankle with my right hand, straighten his leg across my chest, drop to my back, and drive my left foot into his right leg to separate his legs and make it more difficult for him to counter my submission.

Turning onto my left side, I pinch my right knee over Dave's left leg, pull his heel toward my chest, and bridge my hips into his knee. It is important to notice that his toes are to the right of my head and I'm applying outward pressure in the exact opposite direction that his toes are facing. This allows me to hyperextend his leg.

OMOPLATA SWEEP TO SIDE CONTROL ★BJ FAVORITE

As you now know, your opponent's most common means of escaping the omoplata is to execute a forward roll over his trapped shoulder. So far, I've demonstrated how to use that escape to transition into a straight arm bar and a knee bar. In this sequence, I offer another technique to counter your opponent's primary omoplata escape, but instead of transitioning into another submission, you reverse him and establish the top position. To execute this technique properly, you want to turn your body away from your opponent and come up to your knees as he rolls to his back. This creates a pathway for him to complete his roll. Once he lands on his back, turn into him and establish the side control position. This is an excellent technique to have in your arsenal when you are first building an omoplata system because very little risk is involved.

I've established the standard omoplata position. I have my left hand posted to keep my body upright and I have my right arm hooked over Dave's back.

Dave drops down to his left shoulder and begins a forward roll. Sensing that he will overpower my trap on his body and put my right arm in danger, I turn my body away from him, unhook my legs, place my left leg flat on the mat, and pull my right arm off his back.

As Dave begins his forward roll, I continue to turn my body in a counterclockwise direction, post my right hand on the mat, and come up to my knees.

With my body now turned away from Dave, I place both of my knees on the mat, dramatically increasing my chances of obtaining the top position.

As Dave comes down onto his back, I push off the mat with both hands and begin turning my head and body in a clockwise direction. Notice how Dave's left arm is still trapped between my legs.

Continuing to rotate in a clockwise direction, I drive my weight into Dave.

As I continue to drive my weight into Dave, I step my left leg over his left arm. By quickly driving into him, I prevent him from elevating his legs and putting me into his upside-down guard.

I plant my left knee on the mat, push Dave's left arm toward his head using my right knee, hook my left arm around his left hip, and place my right elbow on the right side of his body. It is important to notice how I spread my knees wide to help stabilize the position.

OMOPLATA TO BACK TRANSITION ★ BJ FAVORITE

The first thing I do when I establish the omoplata position is attempt to finish the shoulder lock. If I can't get my opponent to tap, then I will use my positioning to attack his elbow or wrist. If a submission isn't possible, then I'll look for a sweep. In this scenario, your opponent is on all fours and none of your attacks are working. Instead of holding on to the omoplata position, you utilize the sneaky technique demonstrated below to transition to his back. It's not a technique that is used very often, but that's a major part of why it's so effective.

I've established the omoplata position. My right hand is over Dave's back to prevent him from rolling, and my left hand is posted to keep my weight forward. However, it is important to notice that I have not crossed my legs and my control over his arm is not tight.

Due to my lack of tight control over his arm, Dave bends his left elbow to create a gap between my right leg and the back of his arm. Before he can use this gap to pull his trapped arm free, I drive my left heel into the back of his arm to create even more space, and then wedge my left foot over his left arm.

Having wedged my left foot over Dave's right arm and underneath his body, I post my left hand on the mat, post my right hand on his back, and then begin elevating my body.

Supporting my weight on my hands and left foot, I begin swinging my right leg over Dave's body.

I reposition my right leg on Dave's right side and then hook my right foot to the inside of his right leg. At the same time, I hook my left foot to the inside of his left leg. To secure the back position, I hook my right arm underneath his right arm.

SECTION FIVE
SWEEPS AND TRANSITIONS

SWEEPS AND TRANSITIONS

Throughout the book I've demonstrated several sweeps that can be executed off submissions such as straight arm bars, omoplatas, and triangles. This section is devoted to the sweeps and transitions that can be implemented directly from the closed guard. As you will soon see, the majority of these techniques are executed when your opponent stands up in your closed guard. In order to be successful, it is important to execute your sweep while your opponent is in transition. The goal is to hit him when he is most vulnerable, which is when he's in motion or en route to the standing or kneeling position. If you allow him to settle his base, sweeping him to his back becomes much harder to manage. To cover the various closed-guard positions, I've broken this section into three subsections. The first subsection focuses on sweeping a kneeling opponent. The second subsection covers sweeping your opponent when he has one foot planted on the mat, and the third subsection concentrates on sweeping a standing opponent. Although it is optimal when you can sweep your opponent before he can post one foot on the mat or climb to his feet, it isn't always possible. For this reason, I suggest spending time studying all three sections.

SIT-UP SWEEP TO MOUNT

The majority of the time when you sweep an opponent to his back, a battle will ensue to obtain the top position. The nice part about this technique is that it takes you straight to the mount. With all of your weight immediately dropping down on top of your opponent, it makes it very difficult for him to scramble. However, the technique requires speed and precise movements, making it very important to drill on regular basis. If you choose instead to drill only the more elaborate sweeps, you will be missing out on one of the most functional ways to reverse your opponent and obtain a dominant position.

As Dave postures up in my guard, he establishes a right grip on my collar and a left grip along my waistline.

Turning toward my right side, I post my right elbow on the mat and grab the top of Dave's left shoulder using my left hand. Notice how my actions cause his posts on my chest to weaken.

Pulling my body close to Dave's body using my left hand, I post my right hand on the mat, open my guard, place my left foot flat on the mat, and drive my right leg into his left hip. With his posts shattered, Dave grabs my waist and attempts to shove me down to my back.

Using my posts, I drive my hips into Dave's chest and begin turning powerfully toward my right side. Notice how I have dropped my right foot to the mat to help aid in the rotation.

As I drive my hips into Dave's chest, his body becomes attached to my body and his knees rise off the mat. Keeping a tight right grip on his shoulder and continuing to rotate my hips toward my right side, he begins to collapse to his back.

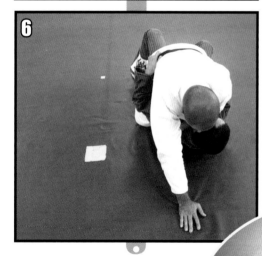

Dave collapses to his back and I follow him over to claim the mount position. To prevent him from bridging and making a quick escape, I keep my right hand posted and continue to pull him into me using my left grip on his shoulder.

STANDING IN POSTURE ★ BJ FAVORITE

Standing in posture is one of the most important techniques in jiu-jitsu, and although it is taught at most academies, it does not receive the attention that it deserves. If you are having no luck with your sweeps and submissions, instead of remaining in closed guard and getting dominated, utilize this technique to escape back to your feet and level the playing field. While it is certainly important to continue to evolve your game with new and improved techniques, it is just as important to bring your foundation with you. And this technique should be a part of every jiu-jitsu practitioner's foundation. In this particular sequence, I demonstrate how to escape back to your feet when your opponent counters the sit-up sweep by driving his arms into your chest. In order to be effective with this move, you must make your transition the instant he moves to flatten your back to the mat. If you wait until your back is already pinned, the technique won't work.

As Dave postures up in my guard, he establishes a right grip on my collar and a left grip along my waistline. Immediately I grab his sleeves.

Turning toward my right side, I reach my left arm over Dave's right arm and grab his left collar.

Continuing to roll toward my right side, I use my left collar grip to pull myself up to my right elbow.

Still pulling myself up using my left collar grip, I post my right hand on the mat, open my guard, and place my left foot on the mat.

As I elevate my hips into Dave's body and continue to turn toward my right, I straighten my left arm. This gives him the room to push me away from him using his arms, which is a common reaction when defending against the sweep. However, in this case I will use the distance he creates to escape back to my feet.

Quickly shoving Dave with my left arm, I support my weight on my right hand and left foot and begin pulling my right leg behind me.

Using my left collar grip to maintain distance, I plant my right foot on the mat behind me and begin to stand. By increasing my elevation, I have also increased my options. From here, I can do a number of different things, such as escaping back to my feet or shooting in, taking Dave down, and assuming the top position.

SIMPLE SWEEP TO MOUNT

This is another invaluable sweep that allows you to reverse your opponent and claim the mount position. While the sit-up sweep requires you to maneuver your body around your opponent's posted arms and obtain body-to-body contact, this one does not, making it an excellent tool for when you're unable to break your opponent's posture. If you look at the photos below, you'll notice that in this particular case my opponent has one foot posted on the mat. Although the sweep is easier to manage when your opponent has one leg up, it is not mandatory for the technique to work.

As Dave postures up in my guard, he establishes a right grip on my collar and a left grip along my waistline. Immediately I grab his left sleeve with my right hand and his right collar with my left hand.

Dave posts his right foot on the mat and begins to stand. In order to be successful with my sweep, I must act quickly.

Rolling over my right shoulder, I bridge my hips off the mat, scoot my hips away from Dave to create space, make my left leg heavy on his right hip, and relax my right leg.

As I come down on my right side, I slide my left knee across Dave's hips and hook my left foot around his right hip. At the same time, I connect my right calf with his left knee. It is important to note that if you do not create enough space in the previous step, your opponent will be able to dump his weight forward and keep you trapped in guard.

Using my grips to pull Dave on top of me, I scissor my legs. This is accomplished by driving my left leg into his right hip and driving my right leg into his left knee where it meets the ground. The combination of these actions disrupts his balance and forces him toward his back. However, it is important to mention that when executing this step you don't want your opponent too far away or too close. You want him close enough so that his legs are light, allowing you to execute your scissor, but not so close that he can drive his weight down on top of you and pin your back to the mat.

I drive my left knee toward the mat, causing Dave to collapse onto his left shoulder. Continuing to scissor my right leg into his left leg to keep it off the mat, I post my right elbow underneath me.

As Dave rolls onto his back, I use my posted right elbow to push myself on top of him and hook my legs underneath his legs to secure the mount position.

I drop my hips to increase downward pressure, wrap my left arm around Dave's head, and post my right hand to stabilize the position. The last step is very important because when your opponent first lands in the position, he will most likely attempt to scramble to escape. If you don't immediately stabilize the position, his chances of accomplishing his goal increase dramatically.

SIMPLE SWEEP SETUP TO HOOK SWEEP

In this sequence, my opponent is postured up in my closed guard and plants one foot on the mat to stand. Immediately I attempt to reverse our positioning by executing the simple sweep, but he counters by pulling his body away from me, which allows him to plant his weight on his heels and increases his base (as a rule of thumb, when you pull your opponent forward so that his weight is on his knees, his base is weaker than when he has his weight on his heels). Although my opponent's redistribution of weight makes it difficult for me to execute the simple sweep, it allows me to transition into the hook sweep. To accomplish this, I hook my foot underneath his posted leg, lift his weight upward, and then pull him forward. Once his body is repositioned directly above me, I have my leverage back and can kick him over to his back with ease. The hook sweep doesn't land me in the mount position like the simple sweep, but it puts me on top, which is more favorable than being on my back.

As Dave postures up in my guard, he establishes a right grip on my collar and a left grip along my waistline. Immediately I grab his left sleeve with my right hand and his right collar with my left hand.

Just as in the previous technique, Dave posts his right foot on the mat with the intention of standing up.

Turning toward my right side and scooting my hips away from Dave, I make my left leg heavy on his right hip and relax my right leg.

Continuing to turn toward my right, I drive my left foot into Dave's right hip and my right leg into his left knee.

Because I have failed to elevate my hips, Dave's base is still sturdy, allowing him to reach his right arm under my left leg. To prevent him from elevating my left leg and passing my guard by moving his body underneath it, I must transition to the hook sweep.

I relax my left leg, circle it around the outside of Dave's right leg, and then hook my foot in the crook of his leg. Notice how my left knee is pointing upward.

Having established my hook, I use my grips to pull Dave toward me. The goal is to get his torso directly above mine to make his legs as light as possible.

Having redistributed Dave's weight off his legs, I drive my right leg into his left knee and kick his right leg upward using my left hook. At the same time, I pull with my right sleeve grip and push with my left collar tie. These actions cause him to collapse to his left side. Immediately I post my right elbow on the mat.

I use my posted right elbow to sit up and follow Dave's body.

Sitting all the way up, I achieve half guard. To prevent Dave from pulling his right leg away from me and standing up or locking me in his closed guard, I spread my knees and center my weight over his left knee.

KNEE-THROUGH SWEEP

When you have an opponent in your closed guard, he will sometimes slide one knee between your legs and apply outward pressure in the hopes of breaking open your guard. Instead of giving into this pressure and allowing him to accomplish his goal, execute the knee-through sweep. If he slides his right knee between your legs, as my opponent does in the photos below, grab his right sleeve with your left hand and establish a right grip on his left pant leg. This gives you control of both his upper and lower body and allows you to break his posture by pulling him forward. Once his chest is collapsed down onto his elevated knee, his posture will be very weak. To get the sweep, all you have to do is roll him toward his right. With his right knee trapped between your legs and his right arm controlled by your sleeve grip, he will be unable to block the sweep by posting his hand or foot on the mat. Techniques like this one are invaluable because they allow you to capitalize on your opponent's offense.

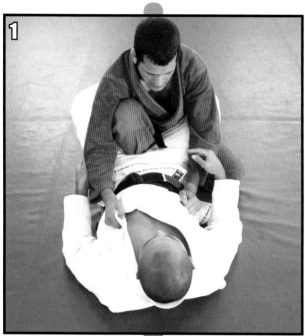

In an attempt to open my guard and pass, Dave slides his right knee between my legs. To set up my sweep, I grab his right sleeve with my left hand.

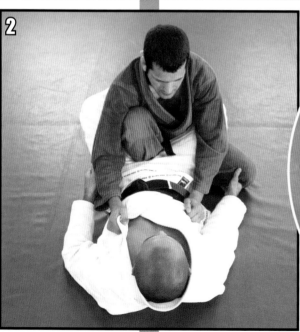

Pinching my knees tightly together to prevent Dave from sliding his right knee forward, I grip his left pant leg on the inside of his knee using my right hand.

Using my legs and left hand, I pull Dave forward to disrupt his base.

Having redistributed Dave's weight with my previous actions, I jerk his leg toward me using my right hand, and pull his right elbow toward me using my left grip to prevent him from posting his hand on the mat. At the same time, I turn toward my left side, causing him to roll to his back.

As I turn into Dave and open my guard, I punch forward with my right hand and pull with my left hand, turning his body circularly to ensure that he ends up on his back.

I continue to punch forward with my right hand and pull with my left. Once I've forced Dave onto his back, I release my grip on his right sleeve and post my left hand on the mat. Using that post, I push my body upright and center my hips over his body.

I release my grip on Dave's right leg and wrap my right arm around the back of his head. His only defense to prevent me from passing his guard completely is his right knee, which is angled upward. To kill all power on his right side, I drive my weight forward, forcing his right heel into his buttocks. From this position, I am in a prime position to pass his guard.

POSTURE BREAK TO OVER-THE-HEAD SWEEP

When your opponent stands up in your closed guard, the split second before he posts his second foot on the mat, he is extremely vulnerable to a forward pull. To capitalize on this vulnerability, pull his elbows to the outside of his body to shatter his posts, open your guard, hook your feet around his waist, and pull him forward using your hip flexors. When timed perfectly, your opponent's body will collapse forward onto your knees and his head will fall to the mat. To cast him all the way over to his back and claim the mount position, pinch your knees together, bridge your body into him, and follow him over. Ralph Gracie had us practice this technique over and over to master the timing, and I strongly suggest you do the same.

As Dave postures up in my guard, he establishes a right grip on my collar and a left grip along my waistline. Immediately I grab his sleeves above his elbows, securing double elbow control.

Dave posts his right foot on the mat. Since I have already established double elbow control, limiting his options, I realize that he will shortly post his left foot on the mat to stand.

Supporting his weight on his right leg, Dave attempts to post his left foot on the mat. Before his foot touches down, I open my guard, position my knees in front of his chest to maintain separation between our bodies, relax my feet, and pull him toward the back of my head using my grips. Since I acted before he posted his foot on the mat, his base is lost and his body comes forward. With this step, it is mandatory to be explosive with your movements.

Using both my arms and legs, I continue to force Dave's body behind me, causing him to fall onto his head. As he goes over, I roll with him, keeping my hips square with his.

I have forced Dave's body into a vertical position. To cast him over to his back, I bridge my hips into him, driving his lower body over his upper body.

I follow Dave's body as he is forced onto his back. As I come down into the mount, I stabilize the position by wrapping my right arm around the back of his head and posting my left hand on the mat. Notice how my feet are hooked underneath his legs.

DOUBLE FOOT-GRAB SWEEP

This is another sweep that you can utilize the instant your opponent stands up in your closed guard. It's very traditional, yet highly effective. Instead of forcing him into a forward roll, you grab his feet with your hands, open your guard, pinch your knees together along his belt line, and drive into him, causing him to fall to his back. The key to success is grabbing his feet the instant he stands. If you delay, your opponent will most likely reposition one foot behind him to increase his base, making it difficult to secure both of his feet.

As Dave postures up in my guard, he establishes a right grip on my collar and a left grip along my waistline. Immediately I grab his sleeves.

Dave posts his right foot on the mat. Realizing that his goal is to stand, I prepare to attack.

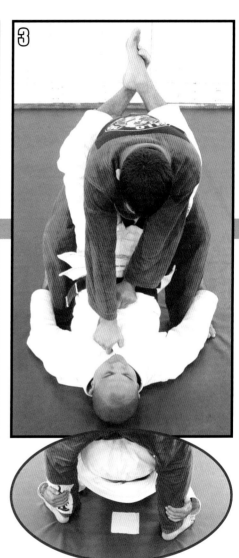

The instant Dave posts his left foot on the mat and stands, I release my sleeve grips and grab both of his heels. It is important to mention that I'm pulling my elbows toward my body. If you angle your elbows outward, your opponent will have a much easier time pulling one foot free and posting it behind him to increase his base. The goal is to keep his feet trapped so that he remains square with your body.

As I grab Dave's heels, I open my guard and pinch my knees together directly underneath his belt line. At the same time, I hook my feet around his back. Once accomplished, Dave can't pull away or drive forward, allowing me to control the distance between us.

As I pull Dave's heels toward my head using my hands, I bridge my hips and drive into him with my knees.

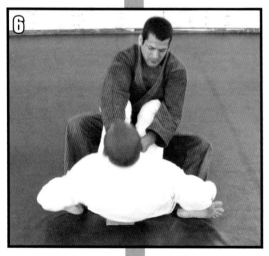

As I continue to drive into Dave with my knees and pull his feet toward my head, he collapses to his butt. Using the momentum generated by the sweep, I begin sitting upright to claim the top position.

Maintaining control of Dave's legs, I sit all the way up and lean slightly to my right. If I were to keep my body square, my legs would act as barriers, making it more difficult to claim the top position.

I post my right hand to the right of Dave's left foot and grab his left collar with my left hand. It is important to be speedy with these steps to prevent your opponent from using his legs to defend your transition.

I push off the mat with my right hand, pull my body forward using my left collar grip, and drive my hips toward Dave's belt line.

As I obtain the mount position, I maintain my left collar grip to threaten Dave and take his focus away from escaping.

FEET-ON-HIP SWEEP

When an opponent is about to stand up in your closed guard, oftentimes he will post his hands on your chest and straighten his arms to maintain a solid base. If faced with this scenario, latch on to his sleeves with both of your hands. This prevents him from elevating his head as he climbs up to his feet. The moment he stands up in your guard, place your feet on his hips, kick him up and over your head, and then execute a backward roll to claim the mount position. The two critical elements of his technique are to pin your opponent's hands to your chest to prevent him from posturing, and to elevate him off the mat the moment he stands. If your timing is off by a split second, then this sweep will fail.

As Dave postures up in my guard, he establishes a right grip on my collar and a left grip along my waistline. Immediately I grab his sleeves.

Dave posts his right foot on the mat. Realizing that his goal is to stand, I mentally prepare to open my guard and attack.

Dave plants his left foot on the mat and stands up.

In one quick movement, I open my guard, draw my knees toward my chest, and then plant my feet on Dave's hips. Notice how my heels are pointing inward, while my toes are pointing outward.

I pull Dave's sleeves toward my body using my hands and kick my feet upward toward the back of my head.

Once Dave's feet are off the mat, I cast him into a forward roll by pulling his arms toward my legs and kicking his butt up and over his head using my feet.

As I force Dave into a forward roll, I turn my head toward my right shoulder to avoid injuring my neck, roll over my left shoulder, follow his hips with my feet, and maintain tight grips on his sleeves. The goal is to connect your hips to your opponent's hips as quickly as possible. The longer this takes, the better chance he will have to scramble and escape the mount position.

I land in the mount with my right foot on the mat. With my hips positioned directly over Dave's, he will have a very difficult time escaping. It is important to notice that I still have control over his sleeves, which will allow me to immediately apply an arm bar on his right arm.

LEG-HOOK SWEEP

This is another sweep that can be utilized when an opponent stands up in your closed guard. If you look at the photos in the sequence below, you'll notice that the instant my opponent plants his second foot on the mat, I gain control of the left side of his body. I accomplish this by hooking my right arm around his left leg and grabbing his left sleeve with my left hand. To execute the sweep, all I do is drive him backward and toward his left side. Unable to step his left leg backward or post his left hand on the mat due to my control, he cannot block the sweep. I strongly suggest learning this technique because in addition to being a highly effective sweep, the initial control opens up other attacking options, such as the arm bar transition shown in the following sequence.

As Dave postures up in my guard, he establishes a right grip on my collar and a left grip along my waistline. I immediately grab his sleeves.

As Dave begins to stand by posting his right foot on the mat, I begin setting up the leg-hook sweep by reaching my left hand over his right arm.

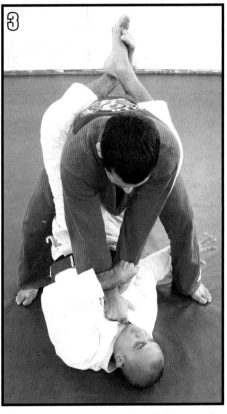

The instant Dave posts his left foot on the mat and stands up, I grab his left sleeve with my left hand, release my right grip on his left sleeve, and hook my right arm around the inside of his left leg. Notice how by keeping my guard locked tight, my hips have elevated off the mat.

In control of Dave's left arm and left leg, I roll onto my right shoulder. Next, I pull my right arm away from his left leg to create some distance, and then chop my arm into the back of his calf, causing his foot to slide along the mat toward my head. If you pull your opponent's leg instead of striking your arm into it, you will not get the desired results.

By chopping my right arm into Dave's left leg I have made his foot turn onto its side and slide toward my head. This destroys Dave's base and causes him to begin falling toward the mat. Since I am still in control of his left arm, he will be unable to post his left hand on the mat and block the sweep.

As Dave falls, I keep my guard closed. Although it may feel more natural to open your guard, that would give your opponent a chance to scramble and escape. You want to keep him controlled tightly between your legs.

As Dave falls onto his left side, I use the momentum of the sweep to post my right elbow on the mat and increase my elevation by driving my head upward. It is important to notice that I am on my side. If your opponent is on his side and you attempt to sit straight up, you increase the chances of injuring the foot trapped underneath his body.

I post my right hand on the mat and push my body upright. At the same time, I open my guard so that when I position my weight over his body, his back won't crush my feet.

Maintaining my cross-sleeve grip, I sit upright and position my weight over Dave's body. To stabilize the mount position, I post my right hand on the mat above his head.

LEG-HOOK SWEEP TO ARM BAR

In Brazilian jiu-jitsu competition, any time you sweep your opponent and obtain the top position, you score points. Not wanting to give you those points, your opponent will most likely scramble to prevent the position change. During this scramble, your opponent will often make critical mistakes. In this sequence, you execute the leg-hook sweep and your opponent drives his arms into you in order to maintain distance and retain the top position, creating the perfect opportunity for you to lock in a straight arm bar.

As Dave postures up in my guard, he establishes a right grip on my collar and a left grip along my waistline. Immediately I grab his sleeves above his elbows.

Dave posts his right foot on the mat and begins to stand.

As Dave posts his left foot on the mat and stands up, I reach my left hand over his right arm and establish a grip on his left sleeve.

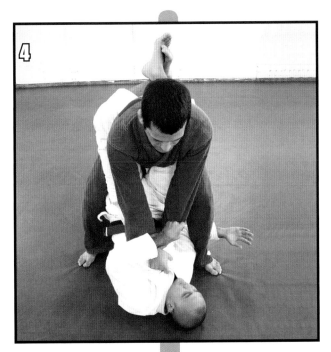

I release my right grip on Dave's left sleeve and hook my right arm around the inside of his left leg.

Just as in the previous technique, I chop my right arm into Dave's left leg, causing him to fall toward his left side. As I am maintaining my left grip on his left sleeve, he is unable to post his left hand on the mat and block the sweep.

As Dave collapses to his left side, I keep my guard closed, post my right hand on the mat, and begin sitting up into him.

As I sit up into Dave, he attempts to prevent me from establishing the mount by pushing on my chest using his arms. Although this makes it difficult for me to claim the mount, it creates an opportunity to apply an arm bar. To set up the submission, I continue to drive my hips forward to straighten his arms. At the same time, I rotate my upper body in a clockwise direction so I can position his right arm down the length of my chest.

When executing an arm bar, I would normally position my left leg underneath Dave's head, but with his head already posted on the mat, there is no room. To deal with this scenario, I slide my left knee over his back and post my left shin on the back of his head. Once accomplished, I use my left knee to shove his head away from his right arm, making it easier for me to attack it. To apply the submission, I keep his right arm pinned to my chest using my left hand and bridge my hips into his elbow. It is important keep your body elevated off the mat using your right hand. The more elevated you are, the more you can hyperextend your opponent's elbow.

LEG-HOOK SPIN

This technique begins just like the previous two—your opponent stands up in your guard, and you hook one arm around his leg and grab his rear post with your opposite hand. As you know, the leg-hook sweep is an excellent submission to execute from this control position, but when up against an opponent who is an expert at defending against the more traditional techniques, utilizing the leg-hook spin is a good way to catch him off guard. The technique requires some acrobatics, but once you get your body moving, you generate a lot of momentum and make it very difficult for your opponent to counter.

As Dave postures up in my guard, he establishes a right grip on my collar and a left grip along my waistline. Immediately I grab his sleeves above his elbows.

Dave posts his right foot on the mat and begins to stand.

As Dave posts his left foot on the mat and stands up, I reach my left hand over his right arm and establish a grip on his left sleeve.

I release my right grip on Dave's left sleeve and hook my right arm around the inside of his left leg.

Instead of attempting to punch Dave's left leg off the mat using my right arm as I did in the previous technique, I grab his left sleeve with my right hand. Once accomplished, I can keep his left arm and leg trapped together using my right grip.

Keeping my right grip tight, I open my guard and kick my left leg over my head toward the mat. To help execute this roll and protect my neck, I post my left hand on the mat and push off.

Continuing to push off with my left arm, I drop my left foot to the mat.

I drop my right foot to the mat, placing Dave's left arm between my legs.

I continue with my roll by dropping my hips toward the mat and elevating my head. With Dave's left arm trapped between my legs, his left shoulder also gets pulled toward the mat, causing him to begin falling toward his back. When executing this step, it is important to use the momentum of your roll to get your hips down and head up. If you pause and slow your momentum when your feet touch down, it will be much harder to drag your opponent down.

Pushing off the mat with my left hand, I posture up and drop my butt to my heels. Once up, I grab Dave's left leg with my left hand so that I can release my right grip and free up my right arm. It is important to notice that my knees are spread wide to increase my base.

I release my right grip on Dave's left sleeve and drive my weight into his body. With my goal being to establish side control, I clear a space for my body by pushing his left knee out of the way using my left arm.

With my hips already turned to the side, I simply drop my right hip to the mat. To secure side control, I drive my weight into Dave's chest, maintain control of his left leg using my left hand, and hook my right arm underneath his head.

INSTRUCTIONAL BOOKS

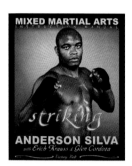

MIXED MARTIAL ARTS INSTRUCTION MANUAL
ANDERSON SILVA

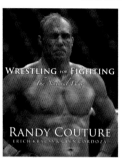

WRESTLING FOR FIGHTING
RANDY COUTURE

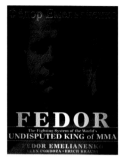

FEDOR
FEDOR EMELIANENKO

MASTERING THE RUBBER GUARD
EDDIE BRAVO

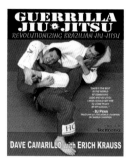

GUERRILLA JIU-JITSU
DAVE CAMARILLO

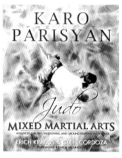

JUDO FOR MIXED MARTIAL ARTS
KARO PARISYAN

THE X-GUARD
MARCELO GARCIA

MASTERING THE TWISTER
EDDIE BRAVO

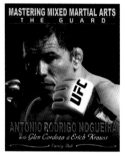

MASTERING MIXED MARTIAL ARTS
ANTONIO RODRIGO NOGUEIRA

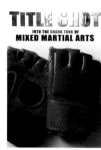

TITLE SHOT
KELLY CRIGGER

JIU-JITSU UNIVERSITY
SAULO RIBEIRO

MACHIDA-DO KARATE FOR MIXED MARTIAL ARTS
LYOTO MACHIDA

JACKSON'S MIXED MARTIAL ARTS: THE STAND UP GAME
GREG JACKSON

DIRTY BOXING
MATT LINDLAND

DVDs

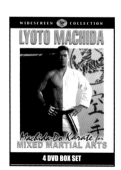

MACHIDA-DO KARATE FOR MIXED MARTIAL ARTS
LYOTO MACHIDA

GUARD FOR MMA
ANTONIO RODRIGO NOGUEIRA

HALF, INSIDE HOOKS, & DOWNED GUARD FOR MMA
ANTONIO RODRIGO NOGUEIRA

PASSING FOR MMA
ANTONIO RODRIGO NOGUEIRA

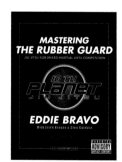

MASTERING THE RUBBER GUARD (DVD)
EDDIE BRAVO

RELATED BOOKS BY BJ PENN

Mixed Martial Arts: The Book Of Knowledge
by BJ Penn with Erich Krauss & Glen Cordoza

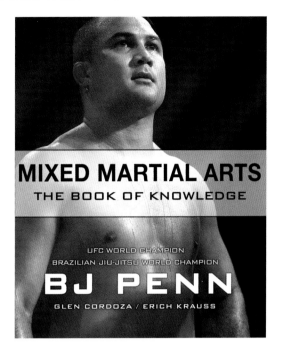

TITLES SOON TO BE RELEASED IN BJ'S "BOOK OF KNOWLEDGE" SERIES

Brazilian Jiu-Jitsu: The Open Guard
by BJ Penn with Erich Krauss & Glen Cordoza

Brazilian Jiu-Jitsu: Butterfly & Half Guard
by BJ Penn with Erich Krauss & Glen Cordoza

Brazilian Jiu-Jitsu: Passing The Full Guard
by BJ Penn with Erich Krauss & Glen Cordoza

Brazilian Jiu-Jitsu: Passing Butterfly and Half Guard
by BJ Penn with Erich Krauss & Glen Cordoza

Brazilian Jiu-Jitsu: Countering The Pass & Submission Defense
by BJ Penn with Erich Krauss & Glen Cordoza

Brazilian Jiu-Jitsu: Side Control & North South
by BJ Penn with Erich Krauss & Glen Cordoza

Brazilian Jiu-Jitsu: Back & Turtle
by BJ Penn with Erich Krauss & Glen Cordoza

Brazilian Jiu-Jitsu: Mount
by BJ Penn with Erich Krauss & Glen Cordoza

BJ PENN IS THE UFC LIGHTWEIGHT CHAMPION AND ONE OF THE MOST POPULAR MMA FIGHTERS OF ALL TIME. HE LIVES IN HILO, HAWAII.

DAVE CAMARILLO IS A BLACK BELT IN BOTH JUDO AND BRAZILIAN JIU-JITSU. HE IS THE HEAD JIU-JITSU COACH AT THE AMERICAN KICKBOXING ACADEMY.

ERICH KRAUSS IS A PROFESSIONAL MUAY THAI KICKBOXER WHO HAS LIVED AND FOUGHT IN THAILAND. HE HAS WRITTEN FOR THE NEW YORK TIMES AND IS THE AUTHOR OF TWENTY FIVE BOOKS.

GLEN CORDOZA IS A PROFESSIONAL MUAY THAI KICKBOXER AND MIXED MARTIAL ARTS FIGHTER. HE IS THE AUTHOR OF TWELVE BOOKS ON THE MARTIAL ARTS.